Deep Calls to Deep

BRANDON ANDRESS

Cover Design and Interior Layout by Matthew J. Distefano

Print ISBN 978-1-964252-25-4

Electronic ISBN 978-1-964252-26-1

Printed in the United States of America

Published by Quoir

Chico, California

www.quoir.com

To subscribe to *Deep Calls to Deep* weekly readings, visit www.brandonandress.com

For my readers...

CONTENTS

INTRODUCTION
ix

DIVINE LOVE
1

PRACTICES
31

HEALING
69

PEACE
97

MINDFULNESS
129

TRANSFORMATION
163

COMMUNITY
193

EPILOGUE
231

REFERENCES
233

INTRODUCTION

THE PANDEMIC IN THE summer of 2020 crushed me, as it did most people. While I don't necessarily mean that in an entirely physical way, I want to acknowledge the lives lost and the countless others with lasting health impacts. But if the physical toll was the epicenter of that catastrophe, the aftershocks were social isolation, cultural division, and psychological devastation. And there was no way to insulate ourselves from the madness.

I remember, during the early part of the pandemic, feeling a profound weight in my chest. This heaviness accompanied me daily and lingered through restless nights. I mistook it for signs of a heart attack. The overwhelming suffocation eventually led me to my family physician, who diagnosed me with anxiety, something I had never experienced before. However, that appointment and the reality of how the world's chaos affected me was the impetus for a two-and-a-half-year writing journey leading to this weekly meditation book.

If you followed my writing during that time, you might have imagined I was writing to you about my daily and weekly practices as a way to help *you* be more present and mindful. While that was eventually true, I wrote primarily to work through my struggles in those early days. I felt isolated, disjointed, and out of sorts, grappling with a reality that had shifted overnight into something I wasn't prepared for. Fortunately, rhythms and practices I had undertaken during other challenging times in my life ultimately helped ground me and regain my sense of humanity.

The *Deep Calls to Deep* weekly writings, as I called them, reminded me of who I am and what is essential—to be rooted in love and express that love in my daily practices for the betterment of my relationships, community, and environment. And if you joined me on that weekly journey, I hope those writings offered peaceful and quiet reminders of your own goodness and the importance you play in making yourself and the world a better place.

But I have to tell you–suffering always surprises me with what it can bring out of us. And it was no different during the pandemic. While suffering ravages, it simultaneously opens creative doors to help us find ourselves again if we are willing. Suffering is wretched and messy, profoundly sad and disquieting, but also subversively hopeful. That has been my experience, and I pray it has been for you, too.

With all that being said, great ideas rarely emerge alone or in isolation. They are only and always a communal offering.

To that end, I would like to thank the incessant encouragement of my wife, Jenny. She is the reason I have finally edited these *Weekly Meditations* together. She continually believed that a greater audience would benefit from these stories and anecdotes than only offering them online. She is probably right because she is always right. So alas, thirty months, one-hundred and thirty weeks of writing, have been distilled into seven sections, each focused on a specific theme to guide your spiritual journey.

The first section, *Divine Love*, explores the depth and expansiveness of love that can heal and transform our lives. Divine Love is not just an emotion but a profound force that can guide us to more compassionate and fulfilling lives. This section will help you connect with this transformative power.

The following section, *Practices*, offers practical approaches to embody spiritual principles in daily actions. These practices are designed to integrate spirituality into your everyday life, making it more intentional and meaningful. You will find ways to bring your inner values into outward expressions.

Healing provides insights into letting go and finding emotional restoration. Forgiveness is a powerful tool for healing past wounds and moving forward with a lighter heart. This section will guide you through releasing grudges and finding peace.

Peace helps cultivate a calm and centered mind amidst life's chaos. Finding inner peace is essential for well-being in a world of distractions and stress. This section will offer techniques to quiet your mind and center your spirit.

Mindfulness encourages living in the present moment with awareness and gratitude. Focusing on the *here* and *now* can enhance your appreciation for life and reduce stress. This section will teach you how to cultivate mindfulness in your daily activities.

The *Transformation* section focuses on personal growth and change. Transformation is about evolving into the best version of yourself. This section will inspire you to embrace change and see it as an opportunity for personal development.

Finally, *Community* highlights the importance of applying spiritual principles to benefit your relationships and community. Spiritual growth is not just a personal journey; it also involves positively impacting those around you. This section will show how to extend your growth outward to enhance your community.

Each section consists of weekly essays with a reflective question to meditate on throughout the week. At the end of each themed section, you'll find week-long daily reflections designed to help you embody the section's content. To me, embodiment is the key to all of this. We can have all the head knowledge to be more integrated and alive, but it is only helpful if we intentionally live it out. As such, this book is meant to be *read and practiced weekly*, allowing you to immerse yourself fully in each theme and experience gradual, profound personal growth. Whether you read it individually or share the journey with others, I hope these meditations will bring you peace, insight, and a deeper connection to Divine Love.

Peace and Love,

— BRANDON
June 2024

DIVINE LOVE

Week 1

From Muck to Wonder

When Will was four years old, we drove an hour from our house to the Hoosier National Forestry in south-central Indiana. This area is beautifully wooded and hilly, perfect for a young first-time hiker. Will was excited based on how much he talked during the hour-long drive.

When I pulled into the parking area, Will was already out of his seat and excitedly standing by the car. He put on his jacket and asked me to help him with his backpack. I helped him and then put on mine. We were off. It was a cool spring evening, not yet sunset, and everything was exploding to life around us. It was perfect. Will knew it as well.

Every thirty seconds for the next hour (and this is no exaggeration), Will burst out, "For Heaven's sake! This is soooo awesome! For Heaven's sake! This is soooo awesome!"

That may have been one of the greatest moments of my life.

Sure, I was glad Will was off to a great start. But it was so much more than that. In him, I saw who I longed to be as an adult. Even though we walked through miles of thick mud and thorn bushes that lined the trails, Will kept shouting joyfully about his awesome experience.

While I was preoccupied with the mud and thorn bushes, Will was taken by the wonder of it all.

That moment with Will parallels our lives, too. We often get caught up in the mundane, forgetting the enchantment surrounding us—the same enchantment he embraced so thoroughly with his childlike spirit. What I have uncovered over the years is that recapturing wonder is essential for opening our eyes and hearts to new possibilities and seeing the world in different ways.

So, in the same way Will and I stepped onto the trail for our adventure, I invite you to do the same in these pages. Except on this journey, these meditations will serve as your contemplative guides to awaken a much deeper love and possibility.

In these weekly meditations, I hope we will journey together through the muck and mire of daily distractions toward a deeper embrace of wonder guided by Divine Love. I aim to encourage a contemplative spirit that nurtures our inner selves and expands our capacity to love others.

On this winding and unpredictable path of transformation, we will learn to quiet the critical voice and spend time with our wounds. We will discover better daily rhythms and generative practices to cultivate kindness, love, forgiveness, healing, and peace. And we will come to understand that what begins in us can ultimately heal and strengthen our relationships and community.

I am humbled and grateful for you joining me on this beautiful journey.

Question

Reflecting on a moment in your life when you felt a deep sense of wonder or enchantment, how can you bring this sense of wonder back into your current everyday life?

Week 2

More Than An Ocean

I LEARNED SOMETHING WHEN navigating through the vast wasteland of car-sized boulders at 12,750 feet while going up the final ascent to Long's Peak in Colorado.

People are less than microscopic.

As we climbed and then turned back to survey the boulder field 1000 feet below us, our tents had become colored dots in a broken sea of browns.

After hitting the summit, we looked down again. Our tents, once vibrant and full of life, were now mere specks, swallowed by the vastness of the landscape. The car-sized boulders, which had seemed so imposing, were reduced to insignificant grains of sand, tossed about by the figurative waves of the mountain's enormity.

That's as descriptive as I can get in conveying how relatively microscopic a person is on a scale we can only somewhat understand. Because if you can begin to understand how insignificant we are from such a short distance on Earth, then you can appreciate our relative nothingness on a cosmic scale.

What is our size from the moon? Think about it. If you are microscopic from a few miles, what are you from 250,000 miles away?

Or, your size from Mars, which is 34 million miles away? Or, from Saturn, which is 750 million miles away? Or, nine billion miles away from the edge of our solar system? For perspective, the Earth is no longer visible to the naked eye at the edge of our solar system.

What is your size from Proxima Centauri, which is 25 trillion miles away and would take 81,000 years to travel at 35,000 miles per hour to get there?

Or from the edge of our expanding universe, estimated to be 46 billion times 5.8 trillion miles away?

We are nothing.

But, if we dare to believe that this existence has been intricately woven together in love, then is that love not larger and more pervasive than the entire universe? How much more immense and unbounded is this love than the universe's vastness and expansiveness? And if this love is that immeasurable, that unfathomable, and that exhaustively immersive, where do we find ourselves within it?

The truth is that there is no distance we can travel, no depth to which we can sink, no barrier behind which we can hide where that love is not inviting us into its full embrace. Imagine inviting that love to become the center of our being.

Question

When contemplating the vastness of the universe and the enormity of Divine Love, how does this perspective shift your understanding of your place, purpose, and possibility in the world?

Week 3

AN EPIPHANY IN SOUTH HAVEN

I HAD BEEN VACATIONING in South Haven, Michigan. The house where I was staying sat next to a church building. As I went for a run on the first morning, I noticed a sign inviting others to join their morning meditation and centering prayer on Tuesday and Thursday mornings. I decided to go both mornings.

As I entered, I took off my sandals and walked barefoot into the sanctuary. A few attendees had arranged the chairs and pillows in a circle around a candle. I sat quietly and closed my eyes. After a contemplative reading and the ringing of a bell, the room quieted for the next thirty minutes.

Everyone had turned off their phones. Every distraction, save for my lone growling stomach, had been eliminated.

After a few moments of mindless wandering, I began to think about how difficult it is to love– how easy it is for me to love those who are lovable, but how difficult it is to love those who are unlovable. Loving is much less black and white than it is gray, I thought. And loving perfectly does not happen instantaneously or overnight. It is an endeavor we commit to choosing and embodying daily.

This thought made me ponder how one can become more loving in all things and to all people. I wondered how love grows in a person from conditional to unconditional. I despaired, thinking about how complicated this process is and how intentional one must be in this pursuit.

But then I turned to look at one of the stained-glass windows. At the center were grapes on a vine. I immediately remembered Jesus' words from the Gospel of John: "I am the vine; you are the branches. Continue to be present, maintain unbroken fellowship with me, and you will bear much fruit."

That is when it clicked for me.

Our ability to love is finite. But Divine Love continually invites us into the possibility of this love being our center. This unbounded and exhaustively immersive infinite source of love desires an unbroken relationship with us. The goal is to remain connected and present, and our love will grow.

Only Divine Love can break through the clouds that impede our vision and pierce the veil shrouding our true reality. When Divine Love becomes our source, we discover the Divine Image in all things and how we are all intimately connected.

Question

How can embodying Divine Love transform your daily interactions and help you cultivate a deeper, more unconditional love for yourself and others?

Week 4

THE DANDELION STORY

I REMEMBER ONE SPRING when we first moved into our current house.

Mother Nature had kindly covered our backyard in a blanket of yellow dandelions. I despised it. But let me set the stage. My father is an exacting and obsessive caretaker of pristine lawns, and unsurprisingly, I grew up just like him. I detested this loathsome weed that threatened to overrun my vision of a serene and unbroken expanse of green around our home.

Every day, I turned onto the street leading to our new house, and my frustration mounted. Having so many dandelions in my yard wasn't just a mental annoyance; it manifested as genuine physical frustration seeping deeply into my bones.

One Saturday morning, possibly the day I had intended to treat the lawn and eradicate the weeds, our sweet five-year-old Caroline gazed out the window in awe. At first, I wasn't sure what had captured her attention, but it quickly became apparent as she exclaimed, in the most innocent and enthusiastic voice, "Those are the most beautiful flowers I have ever seen, Daddy!"

I sat there in silence. What a blow to the gut. I was utterly taken aback.

Caroline's perspective was a stark contrast to mine. While I saw a bothersome weed in dire need of elimination, she saw a genuine floral masterpiece adorning her very own yard, filling her with amazement and delight. Her innocent and unfiltered view of the world was a revelation to me, a stark realization of how my own deeply ingrained biases and influences had clouded my vision.

This was not just a moment, but a profound turning point in my understanding of how our perspective shapes our reality. It was the first time

I truly grasped the profound impact of our perspective on how we perceive and experience this world, and it left an indelible mark on how I see the world.

Unlike me, Caroline hadn't accumulated years upon years of biases and influences that shaped her outlook on the world, other people, or herself. She could see a world surprising her with the gift of tiny, yellow flowers in her backyard. She could discern the beauty, while my distorted lenses revealed nothing but a hideous curse that required immediate action.

Isn't it remarkable how two individuals can gaze upon the same thing and perceive it so differently?

That may be why most children find it easier to discover those places where heaven and earth overlap, where they encounter perfect freedom and perfect love, and where they uncover the wholeness, completeness, and harmony in all things. It's because they haven't been battle-scarred and wearied by life. They still possess untarnished, wide-open eyes and can perceive the world without the fractured lenses that distort their perception of people, situations, and the world around them.

Children remain receptive to awe and wonder, the inherent goodness in all people and things, and a sense that the only moment that truly matters is the one they live in at that moment.

It's no wonder Jesus said that unless we become like little children, we will never truly experience the embrace of heaven and earth. His words call us to abandon our egos and immerse ourselves in Divine Love, for childlike qualities open our hearts and awaken us to awe and wonder. By becoming humble and ego-less, like five-year-old Caroline, we can rediscover the inherent goodness in all people and things, fostering a profound appreciation for the present moment. This, I believe, is the key to seeing and appreciating the dandelions in our lives.

Question

In light of recognizing Divine Love surrounding you and in all things, what changes can you make to see and appreciate the dandelions in your life?

Week 5

The Beautiful Chaos

I WASN'T HAVING A mid-life crisis in my 30s, nor was I depressed. However, my wife frequently caught me sitting at the dinner table by myself, staring out the window into the backyard. I don't know what I was looking for, but maybe it was joy that eluded me.

It seemed my life was about enduring each day, and I was only happy when anticipating something big or exciting. I battled through each day, hoping for some more significant outcome. My happiness and joy were predicated by what I wanted, believed I deserved, or needed out of life. I was so ignorant of the miracle and mystery in which I lived and breathed, the interconnectedness of all things, the infinite possibilities of each moment.

However, there was a moment when it all started to change for me. I was in the family room after supper with my two young daughters. They were playing with each other on the floor, but it was the kind of playing that grates on a parent's nerves —loud, excessive playing.

Feeling tired from a long day at work and not very well, I wished it was a bit later so I could put them to bed. At that exact moment, something hit me, and I closed my eyes, resting my head on the back of the couch, just listening. I heard Caroline's sweet voice, Anna laughing at her, my wife cleaning up in the kitchen, and Aberdeen, my dog, running around and barking at the girls.

It was complete chaos, but the most beautiful chaos I had ever heard.

Tears ran down my face, and I thanked God. I was there again, in that place. Life was far from perfect, but I was fully present and felt wholly embraced. There was an abundance in that ordinary moment that was deep and overflowing. It was so good.

I felt like Emily Webb from the Thornton Wilder play *Our Town*. Rather than looking back in pain and regret like the young woman for mindlessly missing the treasure of every moment before it was too late, I was resolved to begin living this life to the fullest. At the same time, I resolved to start learning how to see and experience life in its fullness, even when it is challenging, even when it is painful, even when I hurt, even when I want to give up. My life was going to change. My mind needed to change. I needed a new heart. I needed eyes that could see clearly. I longed for happiness, joy, and presence. And at that moment, I knew it was possible in my adult life in ways I had never imagined.

That is where my pursuit began– on the couch in the middle of chaos, in the least likely place to discover joy and gratitude.

Question

Reflect on a moment of unexpected joy in your everyday chaos. How can recognizing Divine Love in such moments influence your appreciation of life's imperfections and deepen your sense of gratitude?

Week 6

A Meditation on
Tomatoes

THIS YEAR, WE MOVED our garden to the southeast corner of our lawn. The southwest corner provided too many hours of shade the year prior. With this transition came work—not the kind of work I do Monday through Friday as a salesman, sitting around talking to anyone who will listen. Instead, this work is hand-to-tool, digging, tilling, and cultivating. In this work, there is connection and rootedness. And somehow, it feels like what we were always meant to do.

We don't grow much at all, but we do grow tomatoes. Now, I'm confident that the calories burned preparing the area are a deficit compared to what I receive from the tomatoes. But I do it for so much more than the nutritional value.

Have you ever looked at a sliced tomato on a fast-food sandwich? It is not red-orange. It is pink. For those of us who eat them on our sandwiches, they are bland and tasteless. They are on the sandwich because there is an expectation that something resembling a tomato ought to be on the sandwich. Yet, it is not a tomato. It is something disguised as a tomato. It is a sliced entity that never received love from anyone, a product of mass production and long-distance transportation. This stand-in imposter is tasteless, juiceless. For the recipient, it is a joyless experience to eat it.

But when you invest your time and effort. When you pick up the tomato stands after the heavy storm and carefully lace the vines back through the structure. When you check on them daily and water them when they look like they need a drink. When you talk to them and express gratitude for being a part of your life in this season. When you finally bring them into your house,

13

wash them, and place them on the sunny windowsill. When you finally slice the dark red tomato with so much juice pouring out from them. You are filled with a sense of fulfillment. You are content. You see the work of your hands and the delight in your toil, and it brings you a deep satisfaction.

If the act of working the land, sowing some seeds, and caring for that which we grow can bring so much satisfaction and delight, it begs the question–how did we ever leave it in the first place? Perhaps, it is the return we all need. Hands back in the dirt. Investment. A way to reconnect with nature, to sow seeds, and to grow something that brings us joy. Maybe, just maybe, this is how we begin to recover in some way, to help heal ourselves.

Question

Reflecting on the story of growing tomatoes, how can you bring a similar sense of awareness and appreciation to experiencing Divine Love in your daily life?

Week 7

An Awakening

"I HEARD WHAT SOUNDED like a choir. Everything around me was singing. The sun. The waves. The trees. Even that little bird that shared its song with me earlier. They were all joining together in one song, Odigo. And I could see the gentle and loving invitation of the waves continually beckoning the rocks to join the song, as they are. That is when it hit me. The invitation is not only for the rocks. The invitation is for everything and everyone. And these waves are all around us. They surround us and patiently wash over us to smooth out our sharp and jagged edges. But they are beckoning us to join creation's song together. Just as we are."

"That is real freedom, Thura," said Odigo. "The ability to see the world as it is without needing to judge it. To see its every part and embrace its frailty and brokenness. To discover its naked beauty and love it anyway, sometimes even despite itself. I'm not sure anyone could have said it any better."

When Divine love is our center, it changes how we see the world and others.

When I speak of Divine Love, I refer to a love that is all-encompassing, unconditional, and beyond human comprehension. It is a love that sees beyond our flaws and differences, embracing us in our entirety. When this Divine Love becomes our center, it transforms our perception of the world and others.

While our egos strive to fragment this life into labels, categories, and hierarchies of rightness and wrongness, worthiness and unworthiness, sacred and profane, Divine Love extends an invitation that transcends our divisions. When Divine Love is our center, it empowers us to live, breathe, and experience this life without fearing or needing to protect every illusory boundary or edge. Within this love, we are intimately connected, united, and one. If only we could awaken to its transformative power.

Divine love transcends our affiliations, hierarchies, identities, nationalities, and cultures.

We are loved, and we love others, despite their label of Protestant or Catholic, religious or atheist, fundamentalist or liberal, Democrat or Republican, or Conservative or Progressive.

We are loved, and we love others, whether Americans, Russians, Chinese, Taiwanese, Iranians, Tutsis, Uyghurs, Ukrainians, or Tibetans.

We are loved, and we love others, whether we identify as legal citizens or illegal aliens, Black Lives Matter or All Lives Matter, privileged or underprivileged, gay or straight, transgender or cis-gendered.

No matter who you are, you are in this love.

And I am convinced that nothing can ever separate us from this love or keep it from becoming our center and our reality. Yes, we may hold differing opinions, but Divine Love rises above our disparities and continues to love us, even in spite of ourselves.

Question

How might Divine Love change how you think about people who are different from you?

Week 8

Joining the Chorus of Creation

The cells of our body regenerate approximately every seven years.

Consider this– every single cell of your body is completely replaced over a span of seven years. This staggering fact, as a nearly 50-year-old man, makes me pause in awe. I am not the same person physically as I was when I was a young boy or even as I was seven years ago. The composition of my body is entirely different. Cells have died, and new cells have been generated. I am constantly a new me. And I have done this nearly seven times in my life!

Unbelievable.

But this isn't true for only humans. It seems to be the natural rhythm of all things. Everything is constantly changing and transforming, dying and coming to life. As I look out the window at this very wintry moment, the grass is brown, and the leaves have fallen. But I know that as daylight grows longer, warmer temperatures arrive, and spring precipitation begins to fall, new life will emerge from the ground and blossom from the trees. This is the awe-inspiring cycle and rhythm we live within.

While it's extraordinary to witness the never-ending physical transformation of all living things, it's also sobering. We can always be changing on the outside while remaining unchanged on the inside. This contrast between external and internal transformation is a powerful reminder of our potential for personal growth and the importance of intentional change.

Day by day, year by year, decade by decade, our cells change, and our bodily composition changes, yet we can stay the same person on the inside the entire time.

Think about that.

While our physical bodies have no choice but to change and transform constantly, we only change on the inside as a matter of our own doing. It is an intentional transformation. We have the power to travel purposefully from one destination to another on this spiritual journey. It does not magically happen. It does not unconsciously occur. If we are to begin to change on the inside, it is a matter of intention.

All of creation has been showing us how it is supposed to be done from the very beginning. It is like a song beckoning us to join the chorus of all creation, telling us there is only one pattern of genuinely growing and transforming. And it is of death and life, not just outwardly, in terms of physical changes, but inwardly, in terms of emotional and spiritual growth. Yet, it is a choice as to whether we join this song with our innermost being. We have the power to stay oblivious and unchanged. Or, we can each begin to open ourselves up to the possibility that we, too, can become something new. The choice is ours.

Question

As you consider your own transformation, how can embodying Divine Love help you let go of what no longer serves you to make space for new growth?

Week 9

LIVING THE BEST DAY EVER

IT WAS WELL PAST his bedtime, but four-year-old, Will, was still wide awake. I escorted him upstairs for his nightly routine of brushing his teeth and using the bathroom. As he relieved himself, he burst out, "This is the best day ever! Right, dad?"

His question, unexpected and profound, caught me off guard.

As I squeezed the toothpaste onto his toothbrush, I found myself grappling with his question. I was drained from an exceptionally long day, not just at work, but also from juggling our kids' extracurricular activities. One was cheering at a basketball game, the other had a swim meet in a different town. My wife and I divided our time that evening. I was exhausted.

Was this truly the best day ever? I pondered. If I said yes, would I be telling the truth? If I said no, what would he think about me?

As I took a deep breath, a realization washed over me. Despite the exhaustion, it had indeed been the best day ever.

I had coffee that morning with my wife and then went to work. I watched my daughter swim. I spent time with my in-laws at the event. I was able to eat supper that evening. I was in excellent health. I came home to a roof over my head. My wife and three kids were all at home that night. I was alive and breathing, taking it all in and appreciating the small things. I believed it. I really did. It *was* the greatest day ever.

"Yeah buddy, this is the best day ever." As he looked me in the eyes, his smile told me he was glad I agreed.

Having a perspective that enjoys the present moment and lives it to the fullest has been a long and winding road for me. I don't know how to do it perfectly at this point in my life. But today, I am thankful that God has used a variety of people and situations along the way to open my eyes and heart to the beauty of every moment.

Question

What simple joys have you overlooked recently, and how can cultivating a habit of gratitude help you recognize and appreciate Divine Love in the seemingly ordinary moments of each day?

Week 10

Embodying Divine Love

DAY 1

Action: Identify a situation in your life where expressing Divine Love feels challenging.

Reflection Question: What underlying fears, beliefs, or past experiences might be contributing to the difficulty in expressing Divine Love in this situation? How do these factors impact your ability to respond with love?

DAY 2

Action: Reflect on what Divine Love means and how it differs from human affection or emotional responses.

Reflection Question: In what ways does Divine Love invite you to see beyond the immediate circumstances and consider the broader context of this challenge? How can this shift in perspective change your approach and response?

DAY 3

Action: Choose a specific situation or aspect of your life where you want to embody Divine Love.

Reflection Question: How do you envision your relationship with yourself and others evolving as a result of embodying Divine Love in this situation? What long-term changes do you hope to cultivate through this practice?

DAY 4

Action: Begin applying your understanding of Divine Love to this relationship or situation.

Reflection Question: How are your thoughts, emotions, and actions being reshaped as you actively practice Divine Love? What surprises or insights have emerged from this practice so far?

DAY 5

Action: Assess and reflect on the outcomes of applying Divine Love in this situation.

Reflection Question: How has your practice of Divine Love influenced your sense of self and your connection to others? What specific changes have you observed in your interactions and relationships?

DAY 6

Action: Make any necessary adjustments in your approach based on your reflections.

Reflection Question: What challenges or obstacles have you encountered in embodying Divine Love, and how can you overcome them? How can you integrate the lessons learned into other areas of your life?

DAY 7

Action: Plan how to integrate this practice of Divine Love into daily life beyond this week.

Reflection Question: What specific practices or routines can you establish to sustain the practice of Divine Love in your daily life? How can you hold yourself accountable to ensure that this focus remains central to your spiritual journey?

WEEKLY WRAP-UP

Reflection: As you reflect on the week's experience, what have been the most significant moments of growth or transformation for you? How can you continue to build on these insights and apply them to other areas of your life and relationships?

PRACTICES

Week 11

PLEASE, MAKE WAY FOR MY EGO

EVERY YEAR, BETWEEN MARCH and August, I work out at the Mill Race Park lookout tower in Columbus, Indiana. I walk up and down this architecturally designed 84-foot tower to train for my backpacking trips each August. For vertically challenged Columbus' cornfield flat terrain at 630 feet above sea level, this is the easiest way to get quick elevation to strengthen the legs.

With only five days before my next backpacking trip to the Wind River Range in Wyoming, a rugged and remote mountain range known for its pristine wilderness and challenging terrain, and being cut off from civilization for over a week, I felt the pressure of my growing to-do list. Not only did I have things around the house to complete, but I also had to pack my food and gear and get in the last few workouts at the tower.

As I ascended each flight with my 35-pound backpack, I saw another person descending the stairs. It was an older gentleman I had met a month prior at the tower. Not wanting to be distracted from my workout, I passed him without stopping but greeted him. My pace accelerated after reaching the top. Descending quickly, I slipped by him again as we exchanged a few empty pleasantries.

I knew he would engage me in a lengthy conversation if I didn't begin climbing again before he reached the bottom. And I had too many things on my to-do list for that kind of time investment. But rather than coming down the final steps, the man stopped and started talking to me, blocking the way.

As I stood there, I couldn't even hear him talk because the voice in my head was louder than his words. *I don't have time to talk. I have a lot to get done today. Why don't you move over so I can slip past you?* The voice spoke louder and even faster, but he didn't move. I took a deep breath, and a much calmer voice said, "Love is patient, Brandon."

Gut punch.

As I finally took a moment to really see the 81-year-old man, I realized the significance of his daily routine. He spoke about how he walks the tower each day, and it dawned on me that for an older man who lives alone, these interactions at the park are the highlight of his day.

Another gut punch.

It is easy to talk about Divine Love as our center, but it is all talk. Without intention or the discipline of constant prayer and centering each moment, my ego—with its self-serving agenda—can quickly become the driving force. Maybe it is the same with you. I invite you to reflect on your own experiences and interactions. When has your ego taken over, and how did you respond? What can you do to center yourself and prioritize love and understanding in your interactions?

Question

Reflect on a recent situation where your ego dominated your interactions. What specific practices or disciplines can you adopt to center yourself more on humility and prioritize love and understanding in similar situations in the future?

Week 12

THE WISDOM OF A CLUTTERED GARAGE

A FEW YEARS AGO, I had a recurring issue. My heart and mind raced out of control, and I could not calm myself down. While I initially thought it was a heart issue, my doctor told me it was anxiety. Maybe it has been the weight of the pandemic, the significant disruption in my daily rhythm, or too much time on social media.

I suspect it was all of them together.

This experience made me realize how I had always taken the health of my *inner self* for granted and how easily I can fall apart when I am not intentionally nurturing my soul.

I should have known better, though.

Over the years, my garage has taught me about the state of my inner self and how I need a plan when facing chaos. My family uses our garage as a holding space for items they eventually want to donate. By spring, I reluctantly survey the chaotic accumulation. By summer, I am overwhelmed and anxious when I attempt to clean it out. To make it more manageable, I focus on a small section in the front left (about 3x3 feet) and only concern myself with that area until it is complete. Then, I move to the next 3x3 section.

This approach helps me avoid being overwhelmed. It also makes the task more manageable while giving me a sense of control and achievement. But it took stepping back from the chaos to find a beginning place.

Considering how the pandemic was ravaging me, I knew that I needed to do the same thing for myself.

Richard Rohr wisely says, "The ability to stand back and calmly observe our inner drama, without rushing to judgment, is foundational for spiritual seeing."

How I care for my *inner self* affects my entire being, from how I see myself and my relationships to how I relate to my community and environment. How I feel about myself is how I begin to feel about everything. When one part suffers, the other parts begin to suffer. However, when one part flourishes, the other parts also start to flourish. Everything is interconnected and integrated.

Question

What chaos in your life do you need to quiet, and what specific practices or disciplines can you adopt to step back, calmly observe yourself, and nurture your inner self?

Week 13

Beyond the Zipper

On a freezing Indiana night in mid-February, I stepped out of my warm car and hurried into the homeless shelter for my nightly volunteer shift. Seeking respite in the lobby, a young woman, temporarily staying at the shelter, sized me up and whispered, "You're fly."

If you're unfamiliar with urban slang, it means, "You're hot."

Naturally, I was taken aback and somewhat embarrassed by her forwardness, mainly since I wore a wedding ring and had never met her. However, I managed to smile, searching for my composure by gazing at the floor before shyly replying, "Thank you, I suppose."

Despite my evident awkwardness, she persisted, whispering a bit louder, "You're fly."

My face, concealed by a graying beard, turned crimson. Any remnants of the cold outside dissipated, replaced by a sweat-inducing warmth. Did they crank up the heat in here? I wondered. Even more uncomfortably, I responded, "Um, alright. Hey, thanks."

My gaze fixated on the floor once more, hiding like a child beneath a blanket, hoping to evade attention. The floor was my blanket—if I continued staring at it, maybe she wouldn't see me.

But she continued to stare. And had one more thing to say.

Now, I humbly admit that when someone speaks to you, it's impossible to distinguish between "you're" and "your." The inability to make that distinction in the moment was the death blow.

I looked up one final time, and in slow motion, her arm extended, finger zeroing in on my midsection.

"Your fly."

Only this time, it wasn't a whisper.

An Artic draft pierced through the exposed gap.

Oh no.

My fly.

I felt like I might die from embarrassment.

It was a fitting end to my day.

Earlier in the afternoon, I had called my work partner, inquiring about how her day was progressing. She casually mentioned sleeping in and running errands, neglecting to inform me that she had taken the day off. Naturally, her response left me bewildered.

After a few silent moments, I mustered a hesitant, "What?"

She eagerly replied, a bit too gleefully, "I'm just enjoying our company holiday today."

Yep. I was the lone soul in the company working on President's Day.

Woof.

It was a tough day, but I learned something profound- the most seemingly insignificant moments can hold immense transformative power, serving as valuable teachers in our lives. Instead of dismissing them as mere mishaps, they can become gifts that foster growth and impart wisdom. In my case, two humbling realizations reminded me of the importance of humility. I may be thinking too much about these small moments, but embracing them as gifts allows us to receive their lessons and experience transformative growth.

In his book *Life Together*, Dietrich Bonhoeffer writes, "We pray for the big things and forget to give thanks for the ordinary, small (and yet really not small) gifts."

He is exactly right. The small things are always the key to the big things, especially in our lives.

Question

Reflecting on a seemingly insignificant moment that taught you a profound lesson, what specific practices or disciplines can you adopt to remain open to and learn from these small but transformative experiences in your daily life?

Week 14

In the Wake of Regret

In Greek mythology, there exists a fascinating deity known as Kairos, the god of opportunity. Picture him as a man in perpetual motion, his feet adorned with wings, always on tiptoe, ready to take flight. A unique feature of Kairos is a solitary hair lock extending from an otherwise bald head. As he passes, there is a fleeting moment when one can seize the lock of hair before the opportunity passes.

Standing in the wake of a missed opportunity is a shadowy, cloaked goddess named Metanoia. Metanoia symbolizes *regret for missing an opportunity*. In that place, Metanoia offers something important as one stands in the wake of a missed opportunity—space to reflect and transform.

Each of us has hundreds of these moments in our lives. We stand in the wake of heartaches and missed opportunities and decide how we respond and who we will be. But sometimes, we are so consumed by the pain we are experiencing that we miss the gift it offers.

From the time I was a little boy, I idolized basketball. Throughout school, I was one of the best players. I never worried about making the team because I knew I would always make it and be a starter. Heading into my senior year, I expected the same.

As our team wrapped up practice one day, the coach blindsided me. He delivered a crushing blow– I would not be on the squad. Believing it was a joke, I laughed, but he didn't. I later found out I was the casualty of small-town sports politics.

That experience destroyed me.

I wish I could tell you I looked within, and it made me a better person at that moment, but I didn't. I carried a heavy burden of hatred and unforgiveness in my heart for years. Living with this wound, I became bitter, angry, and resentful. It was a long and arduous journey to find healing and transformation.

But here is the profound power of *metanoia*. It continually offers a sanctuary for self-reflection and growth as long as we stand in the wake of pain and regret. It allows a person to delve inwardly and assess who they have become. It creates space to search one's motives and impulses. And most importantly, it opens doors for the Spirit to heal us and transform us into something new if we are willing to embrace it.

For me, the wake extended for a couple of decades until I realized I was only hurting myself by holding on to that bitterness. It wasn't easy, but I started to embrace the transformative potential of my painful experience and the opportunity it provided me to grow. Through introspection and a willingness to let go of my resentment, I eventually found a path to healing.

Question

Reflect on a missed opportunity in your life. How has this experience shaped you, and what specific practices or disciplines can you adopt to learn from it and facilitate your growth and transformation moving forward?

Week 15

THE ME I WANT TO BE

AFTER GETTING CUT FROM the basketball team in my senior year of high school, I remember only attending one game that season. As much as I would like to believe that I went to the game for some benevolent reason, I only went to berate the coach.

Sitting in the student section, just fifteen feet from the bench, I booed as loudly as possible when the announcer mentioned his name during team introductions. While I don't remember everything I yelled that night, I know it was an ugly representation of me.

At the time, I foolishly believed my verbal retribution would make me feel better.

It didn't.

Isn't it interesting how we grow up believing that we will feel better if we hurt people who hurt us? We desperately want the other person to experience the same pain. But repaying one evil with another never heals our wounds. It only deepens it and perpetuates our toxicity and destruction.

Consequently, we live out of our wounds because it is easier than sitting with and facing them. Instead of doing the necessary holy inner work to heal from within, we continue to transmit our pain to others, which profoundly affects our relationships and how we see the world.

If I could go back to that time and honestly sit with my pain, I would have uncovered something unexpected. The real reason this experience hurt me so badly was that the coach took away what I idolized. From the time I was a little boy, I had allowed this idol to shape and form my identity. As the years passed, my success and the notoriety that came with it fed my voracious and growing ego.

Getting cut obliterated my ego and left me in the wake of pain and then, ultimately, regret.

As I wrote earlier, the beauty of *metanoia* is that it gives space to breathe and self-reflect in that wake. It allows us to look inwardly and search our motives and impulses to see who we have become. *Metanoia* opens opportunities for the Spirit to heal us and become something new if we allow it.

If we are to heal the wounds we continue to carry and grow beyond the culturally conditioned mindset of repaying evil for evil, we must discover the ever-present gift of *metanoia*.

Question

How have your wounds influenced your relationships or how you see the world? What specific practices or disciplines can you adopt to create space for healing those wounds and fostering personal transformation?

Week 16

FUTURE SELF

NO MATTER YOUR AGE, hang with me until I make my point. I often wonder what kind of man I will be when I am much older, like in my 70s and beyond. You may find this odd, but it's a thought that often crosses my mind. I envision a future where I am more patient than I am now, more kind, more loving, and gentle, and significantly less impulsive and reactionary.

As I look into the future, envisioning a more refined version of myself, I recognize the need to know who I am right now. I am not as patient, kind, loving, and gentle as I aspire to be. Instead, I find myself more impulsive and reactionary than I would like. I embody less of the qualities I strive for and more of the traits I wish to change. However, I see a different version of myself in the future—one who has grown and transformed into the person I aim to become. I'm sure many of you can relate to this, as we all have aspects of ourselves that we want to improve.

Whether you are in your teens, twenties, or beyond, have you ever stopped to think about who you will be in the future? What kind of person you will become? Can you imagine a version of yourself that is more realized, more integrated than your current self? Take a moment to reflect on these questions.

I spent some time pondering these questions over the last year. One of the biggest revelations was that a person does not wake up one day and magically become their idealized version. More specifically, I will not wake up tomorrow and instantly be more patient, kind, loving, gentle, and less impulsive and reactionary. Without intentionality or cultivating those things in my life presently, I will never be the person I visualize in the future.

Do you see what I'm saying?

If we never take a moment to reflect on our flaws and weaknesses and remain blissfully unaware of who we are and where we are going, we can never expect to change. Instead of moving forward, we end up going in circles, just putting one foot in front of the other. If that's all we do, we'll end up in the next stage of life, no different than where we are now. This thought should make us all stop and think. Are we content with staying the same? Or do we want to strive for something more, something better?

If we want to grow and become more than our current selves, we must be intentional and self-aware. In other words, we must ask ourselves, Who am I? and Where am I heading? As Richard Rohr beautifully puts it in his book Falling Upward: A Spirituality for the Two Halves of Life, "When [we] get [our] *Who am I?* question right, all of [our] *What should I do?* questions tend to take care of themselves." Rather than expound on that last line, I will leave it for you to contemplate.

Question

Envision the person you wish to become. What specific practices or disciplines can you adopt now to develop the key traits and habits that will align you with your future self?

Week 17

NAKED

IT IS INTRIGUING HOW humanity's instinctive response was to hide their nakedness. This act of hiding, whether from others or ourselves, has become a recurring theme in our lives, often hindering our personal growth and emotional healing. We hide to keep from being truly, authentically seen.

Of course, I speak metaphorically. But it is no wonder we have such difficulty dealing with our wounds.

We wrap ourselves in busyness. We shroud ourselves in noise and stimulation. We envelop ourselves in distraction. We live fabricated and curated lives to hide (or not have to deal with) what is below. We imagine with each new layer, we will have better lives and be whole, or at least have the appearance of those things. But beneath the veneer and cosmetic application, we neglect the source of our dysfunction- the infected wounds we carry.

A friend of mine astutely asked, a few weeks ago, how to sit with our pain. I imagine our first move is stripping away the artificial layers that conceal our wounds. I stumbled into this wisdom while backpacking over the last decade and a half. While there are other ways to do this, the solitude of backpacking provides an essential stripping.

In solitude, we purposefully distance ourselves from the noise and distractions of our daily lives. We detach from our dependencies and addictions, stepping away from the chaos and the constant need for social validation. In this state of solitude, our masks lose their significance, allowing us to discard them.

Solitude compels us to confront our true selves, leaving no room for hiding. We metaphorically step out from behind our protective barriers and stand exposed. In this state of vulnerability, we see ourselves more clearly, and our emotional wounds become apparent. It is in this raw state that we can truly sit with our pain and decide what to do with it.

Solitude is not a one-time remedy that heals us but a necessary beginning point for the regular rhythm we need.

Question

As you think about patiently transforming your pain rather than continuing to transmit it, what layers do you hide behind that need to be removed, and what specific practices or disciplines can help you embrace vulnerability and begin healing?

Week 18

From Shadows to Sunrise

About fifteen years ago, I was reading *Life Together* by Dietrich Bonhoeffer. He discussed the idea of "confessing our sins to one another" so that we could be "healed." While I can't recall his exact argument, I imagine it involved exposing our dark and hidden parts to our closest friends, who would meet us with Christ's loving and non-judgmental light.

Inspired by this concept, I gathered a small group of my closest friends, shared what I had been reading, and confessed every "sin" I could remember throughout my life. When I finished, I felt light and free, completely unburdened. I offered others the same opportunity, but no one else spoke up. I have never seen so many people stare at the carpet simultaneously (insert laughy-face). The following week, no one showed up. I grin as I recall that moment. Eventually, more people joined, and our confession group continued for another three or four years.

Those moments were some of the most liberating experiences I've ever had. There's something profoundly freeing about being completely vulnerable when you feel loved without feeling judged. And that's how I think about these weekly writings with you. They are a way of continuing that confessional tradition of baring my soul by removing the layers. I feel like I can open myself up to all of you each week because I know I am loved in this place.

Some may think it's foolish to be so public with my failures and misgivings, to be so open about the issues I deal with. Yet, there is something to gain from such openness—both for me and you. Maybe Bonhoeffer was onto something. That's why I continue, regardless of any potential negative perceptions others may have of me. The peace and freedom we seek might lie beyond our "confessions." Furthermore, I wonder if we could alleviate many of our societal problems with greater honesty and transparency among us. Maybe that's the healing we really need.

Yes, I know I'm wildly idealistic. But opening up and allowing ourselves to be truly seen can foster a more compassionate and understanding world and create more genuinely free people. Who knows? We might all find more freedom and connection by sharing our authentic selves, as I did with my friends, breaking bread and pouring ourselves out.

Question

What truths about yourself have you been holding back from sharing, and what specific practices or disciplines can you adopt to foster greater openness and authenticity, thereby enhancing your relationships and personal well-being?

Week 19

A Lesson in Being Hangry

EVEN BEFORE THE WORD *hangry* existed, I discovered the intuitive nature of my body.

As a young man in my twenties, I regularly fasted, or abstain from eating food for spiritual purposes. This discipline quickly taught me how my body communicates when hungry and how that may affect me.

This principle applies to much more than food.

Over the years, I have developed a sensitivity to my body communicating with me. I usually experience a heaviness in my upper chest and lower neck area where my unease usually resides.

Rather than leaving the heaviness unresolved and allowing it to affect me throughout the day, I have learned to talk to it. I ask the heaviness where it came from and why it is with me. In every instance, I can follow it back to something that happened earlier—a conversation that was off, someone being upset with me, or something from my past.

The other day, my daughter shared that she overthinks things to an unhealthy degree. I asked her to go deeper and discover what issue may be causing her to overthink. Considering it further, she supposed her overthinking resulted from anxiety. But again, I noted that her anxiety is a symptom of an underlying issue.

Going deeper, she discovered that her overthinking came from the belief that she needed to perform at the highest level in everything she did. I asked her if this comes from the expectations others have of her or her expectations of herself. She said the latter.

We often perceive these manifestations as the actual problem rather than symptoms of the problem. While having good discipline and healthy life rhythms to center ourselves is always beneficial, we will only discover the underlying issue when we dig deeper.

The same is true for our wounds.

As you listen to your body, what is it telling you? What would it look like to travel to the source? What wound is behind your anger, bitterness, and resentment? What wound is causing your unhappiness? What wound is the root of your impatience and frustration? What wound fuels the judgment and hatred you feel toward yourself or others?

It may be a difficult journey to get there. But once you arrive, the process of true healing may begin.

Question

Take a moment to tune into your body's signals. What are these sensations revealing about your underlying feelings, habits, or unresolved issues, and how might the practice of listening to your body help you address and heal them?

Week 20

Finding Stillness

THE SUN WAS ALREADY blazing in the near-cloudless early morning sky. As we approached Horseshoe Mesa in the Grand Canyon, all but a single, lowly shade tree remained, its sparse branches casting a patchy relief from the scorching heat. We thought it would be the perfect spot for a quick drink and reprieve from the sun's relentless rays before our big climb.

As we stood there, one of the guys asked me if I had any music on my phone. Usually, I clear everything off of it to make room for the pictures I take during the trip. But to my surprise, there was one single song in the queue.

As I pressed play, we all quieted.

In that anticipatory moment, the song *Passing Afternoon* by Iron and Wine sweetly greeted us.

There was an overwhelming intimacy I had never fully experienced through a song, a profound connection that felt like never having heard a song before.

There was an acuteness to every sound, to every word sung. There was a simple yet profound appreciation for every note, every melody, every harmony. For four days, the only sounds we heard were of nature- the blowing winds, the rushing waters, the singing of birds, and each other's voices.

Our solitude silenced the sounds of busyness and distraction. An easing stillness cleansed and refreshed my soul, renewing my appreciation for what I usually take for granted.

I wasn't listening to a song to distract myself, as one trying to fill the void of uncomfortable silence or simply consuming to consume. I was fully present and listening, as if for the first time, with deep appreciation.

In a hyper-stimulated world, something is renewing and refreshing about purposefully removing oneself to find refuge in the stillness and quiet or intentionally abstaining and then slowly reuniting. It is an essential discipline that reminds us of the resident goodness and simple beauty we can all too easily take for granted.

This kind of intentionality moves us from a place of endless addiction and mindless consumption, where we consume music, nature, and even our thoughts without truly appreciating them, to a place of simplicity and beauty. It's a place where we can experience and appreciate all things anew, where every note, every melody, every harmony is a gift to be savored.

Question

What noise or busyness do you need to quiet in your life to be more present with yourself, others, and your surroundings, and how might practicing stillness help you cultivate this presence?

Week 21

ABANDONING THE DOG

IN *THE GOD'S OF the Copybook Headings*, Rudyard Kipling concludes his poem by saying a few things are certain.

"The Dog returns to his Vomit and the Sow returns to her Mire, And the burnt Fool's bandaged finger goes wabbling back to the Fire."

Each instance in Kipling's poem paints a picture of the cyclical nature of folly, implying that a fool will always return to what he knows, even when it is not beneficial. This resonates with me on a personal level, as I often find myself slipping back into a negative, critical headspace that can spiral downward into a black hole. Mentally, I can cyclically wallow in this negative space to my detriment, much like a dog returning to its vomit or a sow returning to its mire.

You may have had that experience, as well.

However, it takes humility to recognize and admit what is destroying you. It takes courage to step away from the cycle and choose a kinder, more generative path.

In understanding that prayer is any interior journey cultivating faith, hope, and love, I must push back the dark clouds surrounding me and create a clearing for this holy inner work.

At first glance, the idea of prayer as an interior journey cultivating faith, hope, and love may seem like a lofty, spiritual exercise. But let me assure you, it's been surprisingly practical and beneficial in my life.

Before any other undertaking, I read one passage from a daily meditation book each morning. While the coffee is brewing, I stretch rather than scroll on social media. And after work, I take a walk outside.

In these tasks, I intentionally do not think about anything from the past or future. I remain fully present, listening to every breath and giving thanks to God for everything I see. Then, at night, I read wise, insightful books that enrich my understanding, connect me with different perspectives, and guide me on this spiritual pilgrimage. Lastly, I have made it a goal to encourage at least one person each week. I want the people in my life to know what good I see in them and how thankful I am for them.

By committing to these mindful, prayerful practices, I slowly dismantle the destructive cycles within me, creating space for peace and gratitude that may transform my life, breaking free from the cyclical folly that Kipling so vividly depicts.

Question

Reflect on a negative thought pattern or habit you return to out of comfort. What specific practices or disciplines can you adopt to actively choose and maintain a healthier path forward?

Week 22

Depletion and Renewal

WRITING IS A DEEPLY emotional journey for me. It's not just about putting words on a page but capturing the deep feelings and emotions within me. When I feel something in my chest, I write. But when that feeling is absent, I've learned to respect the silence over the years and not force the words. If I were to ignore this silence and force myself to write, I often find that the words lack depth and authenticity, and the process becomes more of a struggle than a creative outlet.

This experience is especially true after writing a book. But first, the book-writing process for me is unorthodox. In the beginning, an idea comes to me. The only way I have ever been able to describe it is that it feels like a "download" or that I have been "connected to a flow." I immediately begin taking notes and feverishly writing the ideas. After about a week, the download or flow completes, and I stop taking notes. At that point, I leave the notes to sit for about four to six months and never look at them. Finally, when the time feels right, I revisit everything I have written. This *right time* is often marked by a renewed sense of excitement or a deep longing to continue the story. I know I'm ready to start writing again if I still have the same passion for the idea as when I first wrote everything down.

I do this because writing a book is a marathon. If I start writing a book, I don't want to lose interest halfway through. I have to really feel it.

So when I write for five or six months, every day for hours, pouring out every ounce of my inner being, the process leaves me utterly depleted. When I complete a book, I'm physically drained and emotionally spent. The thought of writing anything else, reading, or even entertaining new ideas is overwhelming and exhausting. I'm always left feeling completely worn out.

But after writing my last book, I did not listen to my body. I took on an editing project for a novel, where I had to review and revise an entire manuscript, wrote two chapters for anthology projects with my publisher, and tried to keep my weekly writings going. As you would expect, after several months, I felt this maniacal schedule catching up with me.

But that's our tendency. We often disregard the profound wisdom of our bodies. We push ourselves beyond our limits, driven by expectations and obligations. And we pay for it with our minds and bodies. Yet, a more holistic approach to life recognizes the need for balance and a healthier rhythm. This means after intense creativity, I must pause and replenish myself, not engaging in any creative activities until I feel restored. Understanding and respecting our body's signals and prioritizing self-care in our endeavors, whether creative or something else, is crucial.

Question

After a period of intense effort or activity, how do you typically unwind and rejuvenate? What specific practices or disciplines can you adopt to more effectively honor your need for rest and renewal?

Week 23

Embodying Practices

DAY 1

Action: Identify an area in your life where you feel stuck in negative patterns or unproductive habits.

Reflection Question: What specific triggers or situations lead you to engage in this negative pattern or habit? How do these triggers influence your thoughts and actions?

DAY 2

Action: Reflect on the underlying causes and triggers of this negative pattern or habit.

Reflection Question: What deeper emotions or past experiences are connected to this negative pattern or habit? How have these underlying factors shaped your current behavior?

DAY 3

Action: Set a clear intention to change this negative pattern or habit into a positive one.

Reflection Question: How will changing this pattern or habit positively impact your overall well-being and relationships? What specific steps can you take to ensure this change is sustainable?

DAY 4

Action: Begin taking concrete steps to replace the negative pattern or habit with a positive one.

Reflection Question: How do these initial changes make you feel emotionally and physically? What support or resources can you draw upon to maintain these positive changes?

DAY 5

Action: Assess the impact of the changes you've made so far.

Reflection Question: What specific positive outcomes have you observed in your daily life as a result of these changes? How have these outcomes influenced your motivation to continue?

DAY 6

Action: Make any necessary adjustments to your approach based on your reflections.

Reflection Question: What obstacles or challenges have you encountered during this process? How can you adjust your approach to overcome these challenges and stay committed to positive change?

DAY 7

Action: Plan how to integrate this new positive pattern or habit into your daily life beyond this week.

Reflection Question: What specific practices or routines can you establish to ensure that this positive pattern or habit becomes a permanent part of your daily life? How can you track your progress and celebrate your achievements?

WEEKLY WRAP-UP

Reflection: As you reflect on the week's experience, what have been the most significant insights or breakthroughs for you? How can you apply these insights to other areas of your life to support ongoing growth and transformation?

HEALING

Week 24

THE CARD THAT BROKE ME

WHEN I WAS IN college and dating Jenny, there was a Friday night when we were planning to hang out. As the minutes and then the hours began to pass, my impatience grew into simmering frustration and eventually overwhelming anger. I was livid that she was taking so long, not answering my phone calls, and seemingly ruining our Friday.

After several hours of waiting in my room with no response, there was finally a knock at my door. And as Jenny walked in, my anger was immediately evident. I was fuming mad and peppering her with a litany of questions.

Where have you been?

What have you been doing?

Why are you so late?

Why didn't you answer my calls?

I didn't listen to anything she said, and no response would have satisfied my anger.

But then, instead of trying to answer my questions, she did something unexpected. She just handed me a card.

And it wasn't just any card.

It was a card she had meticulously, patiently, and lovingly crafted for me over the three previous hours. The card was filled with overwhelming specificity, detailing all the memorable moments we had shared as a couple and expressing how much she loved me. Each word, each memory, was a testament to her love and our relationship.

I got very silent.

Stick-my-foot-in-my-mouth silent.

Let's be honest. It would have been easier for her to withhold the card and break up with me immediately. I did not come close to deserving the card. But Jenny gave it to me anyway, despite my anger and bewilderment, as an act of profound kindness and love.

My anger turned to regret.

Her act of kindness, not her justified retaliation, struck a chord deep within me. It was a wake-up call, a realization of my own shortcomings. Her kindness made me want to change- to be more patient, kind, and loving myself. Despite how I had violated our relationship, her kindness changed my heart.

When kindness confronts us through undeserved mercy, grace, or love, it can be transformative. It has the power to change hearts, to breathe life into relationships, and to inspire us to be better.

Reflecting on this experience, I am reminded of a wisdom that states that the kindness of God transforms the heart. Not the guilt of God. Not the shame of God. Not the threats of God. It is the kindness of God that changes a person from the inside, creating vibrancy and life. In a similar way, Jenny's kindness transformed my heart and our relationship, bringing vibrancy and life to our love.

Question

Reflecting on how undeserved kindness can transform a heart, how might you open yourself to experiencing the kindness of God, and in what ways can this lead to forgiveness and healing in your own life?

Week 25

A Story of Forgiveness

I remember talking to a lady several years ago who had been abused by her father as a young girl and who was, understandably, still dealing with the mental anguish of the abuse as a middle-aged woman. She had reached a point in her life where she no longer wanted to live in the bitterness and anger of her past. And she was ready to forgive her father.

But he had died a decade before.

I explained to her that forgiveness can happen at any time and does not require two people to come together, agree with one another, or accept the other person's forgiveness. The other person does not even need to be alive to forgive them.

Forgiveness is, very simply, a change in one's heart toward another, moving from a place of anger, bitterness, and resentment to a place of compassion and mercy. It is a heart posture that no longer holds enmity, hostility, or condemnation toward another but manifests from a place of compassion and mercy into a loving grace.

Forgiveness is never dependent upon another. It is always self-generative.

That is why forgiveness can never be transactional or an "if you do something for me, then I will forgive you" proposition. It is only, and always, the posture of one's heart toward another. And to that end, forgiveness is always a one-sided affair. It begins and ends with you and you alone.

That understanding of forgiveness was a huge revelation for her (and it may be for you as well), as she could then forgive her father, even though he was no longer alive. Her forgiveness finally released her from the hostility that had consumed her for decades.

Question

Reflecting on the power of forgiveness as a transformative act, what specific steps can you take to forgive someone from your past, and how might this decision lead to healing and freedom in your life?

Week 26

To Forgive a Murderer

I was a junior in high school when a devastating and horrific crime rocked my hometown of Madison, Indiana.

In 1992, four teenage girls (three of whom I went to school with) tortured and murdered a twelve-year-old girl named Shanda Sharer.

It is by far the most heinous and gruesome event I have ever been close to, and there is no way to fully capture how traumatic it was for everyone involved and for our small community. Despite attending the trial and following what I believed was every detail at the time, I recently attempted to listen to a podcast about the murder but had to turn it off. The monstrous details were far beyond what I thought I knew or could handle. It was heartbreaking.

In interviews with Shanda's mother, Jacque Vaught, her eyes were always red and swollen. She looked perpetually broken. As a parent, I don't know how she kept going each day.

About a decade ago, one of our family friends, whose family has a service dog, told me that the "ringleader" of Shanda's murder was working as a service dog trainer while serving her prison sentence. Melinda Loveless became known as one of the best trainers in the Indiana Canine Assistance Network (ICAN) Program at the Indiana Women's Prison.

Intrigued, I began researching and landed on a story by journalist Anne Ryder that I never expected to read.

One of the breeders that supplies dogs to the program became friends with Shanda's mother. The breeder told her about Loveless. However, Jacque never wanted contact with any of her daughter's killers. She said about Loveless,

"If you want to see as close to a person that has absolutely nothing inside of them, look into Melinda's eyes cause there's nothing there."

However, taking the breeder's advice, Jacque agreed to watch a video of Melinda working with the dogs.

Twenty years after her daughter's murder, what she saw in Melinda moved her.

"I was really taken aback," said Jacque. "I saw someone who was almost reborn. Melinda was someone who had learned to nurture something."

Defying all human logic and conventional wisdom, Jacque did something extraordinary. She donated a puppy to the program in Shanda's honor and let Melinda train it.

"[Jacque] helped me to heal, forgive and grow, whether she wanted that or not," Loveless said through tears. "She did a good thing. And I would thank her. I couldn't thank her enough. Angel (the puppy) is in good hands. And I'm doing it for Shanda."

Question

How might forgiving someone who deeply hurt you foster peace and healing in your life, and what steps can you take to move toward this forgiveness?

Week 27

THE KINDNESS OF TED LASSO

THERE IS A REASON why Ted Lasso captured the hearts of millions.

But first, let me give you a brief overview of Ted Lasso. It's a heartwarming comedy series on Apple+ that follows the journey of a college football coach, Ted Lasso. Despite his lack of knowledge about the sport, he's unexpectedly hired by an English football (soccer) team. The twist is that the team's current owner, in an attempt to undermine her ex-husband's legacy, covertly recruits Ted Lasso with the intention of sabotaging the team.

Ted Lasso's character resonates with viewers because of his unwavering kindness, even towards those who may not deserve it. He shows compassion to his backstabbing boss and responds to the fans' jeers with a smile and a wave, refusing to let their negativity affect him.

I know that sounds ridiculous. But it is shocking to see a character on a television series display such radical kindness these days in the face of opposition, hatred, and backstabbing.

However, I believe that is why the show is so popular—we are collectively desperate for kindness. In a world where conflict, retaliation, and the pursuit of power dominate our daily lives, we have a deep-seated desire for a more compassionate and understanding way of being.

My neighbor, Ann Heimann, passed away several years ago from a spinal cord tumor just below her brain stem. She believed this burden made her more kind, caring, and compassionate toward others. Here is a portion of her deeply earned wisdom from her obituary.

Even when it felt like someone wronged her or she was dis-appointed by another's actions, she would come to reconcile that loss by realizing her expectations were greater than what that person could give. This realization provided Ann with a profound sense of understanding and deep peace. She learned it was easy to release any blame and find the return pathway to peaceful and loving relationships.

In many ways, Ted Lasso's story and Ann's wisdom remind us that kindness and understanding, especially when facing difficult people or situations, can transform our lives and the world around us.

Question

Reflecting on a recent situation where you could have responded with kindness instead of judgment, how might choosing kindness in similar situations foster forgiveness and healing in your life?

Week 28

A Necessary Eviction

I HAD A BLACK hole in my chest and a feeling of suffocation. At any moment, I felt like I could start crying for no apparent reason.

A voice told me I was not a good writer. It then progressed by saying that no one cares what I have to say and that what I do is a waste of time. Finally, it told me that no one even likes me.

Trust me, I've been there. In the depths of my own darkness, I allowed that voice to echo, to my own detriment, for far too long.

Have you ever experienced an inner voice that says you are not good enough? An inner voice obsessed with telling you that your actions are a waste of time? An inner voice relentlessly trying to convince you that you are not good? An inner voice determined to make you feel isolated, worthless, and alone?

This voice creeps in when you are on social media. It convinces you that everyone else is living their best life, traveling the world, and having mind-blowing experiences while you are home alone.

This voice tells you to compare your life to those around you. It assures you that your work, art, success, and well-being are not as good as others.

This voice creates million-and-one scenarios where everyone gets together for meals, parties, and gatherings while you miss out.

This voice wants you to believe you are alone and persuade you that nothing is good in you.

And this voice is happy to stay with you as long as there is an open invitation.

My experience proved how subtle and destructive this voice is when we allow it to speak into our lives. It taught me how essential it is to nurture and care for my inner self by filling the void with something generative.

For something to grow, one must first open the soil for something to be sown.

Engaging in centering activities, such as meditation and prayer, is crucial. They create a space within us for something new, something positive. They beckon Divine Love to fill the void and silence the destructive voice.

These "interior journeys," as Richard Rohr describes them, allow us to experience love within ourselves, maybe even for the first time.

Question

Reflect on the destructive inner voices you've encountered. How can evicting these negative thoughts foster a healthier and more forgiving mindset towards yourself and others, and what practices can help you nurture this transformation?

Week 29

Living With the Enemy

I watched a television series by the late Morgan Spurlock called *30 Days* several years ago. The premise was to take two radically different people from ideological extremes (Christian/Atheist, Pro-life/Pro-Choice, etc.) and have them live together for a month.

On the surface, the show appeared to be more shock television than anything else, but there was a beautifully hidden genius in what subsequently transpired in each episode.

I remember one episode vividly. A patriotic, anti-immigration vigilante who volunteered to keep illegal immigrants from coming into the country stayed with a Mexican family living illegally in the United States.

As you can imagine, each was initially fearful of the other. Each had constructed preconceived ideas about the other from their past experiences, biases, and stereotypes. Their initial conversations were like ours today- hostile and argumentative.

But as the days passed, they began seeing each other differently.

They knew what they *should believe* about each other based on the national narrative and what was on paper. However, they began to hear each other's stories through continued conversations and eating together at the table. They slowly changed their perceptions of the other. They discovered the other's hopes and dreams. They began to see each other as human beings navigating the complexities of life. Whether they would have characterized their experience this way or not, they began to see the Divine Image in the other.

In one of the most poignant moments at the end of the show, the border vigilante, nearly in tears, said to the family:

"What I've learned the most here was to understand and receive your point of view directly from you. Because you can read a book, but a book doesn't laugh. A book doesn't cry. A book doesn't have memories. A book isn't a human being. But your circumstances and everything that has happened here is a precious opportunity that has been given to me."

Knowing someone more deeply than the stereotype or the caricature is risky. Having a conversation or a meal with the "enemy" may put you at odds with your own "tribe." Being vulnerable enough to listen and hear another's perspective may take sacrifice on your part. You may still not agree with their perspective in the end. But when love becomes our center, it is the ground upon which understanding can flourish and hearts may change.

Question

Consider someone with whom you have significant differences. How might intentionally seeking to understand their experiences and perspectives foster forgiveness and mutual healing in your relationship?

Week 30

My Friends of Misery

In a previous reflection, I discussed a pivotal moment from my senior year of high school—a devastating cut from the basketball team due to small-town sports politics, which profoundly impacted my spirit and character. As a 17-year-old, I did not know that I could do anything else with my pain than live out of it and transmit it.

As a result, my wound festered.

Rather than attend to the infection, I ignored it and allowed it to become more toxic.

Metallica joined me there. They seemed to understand what I was feeling. James Hetfield sympathetically sang the song, *My Friend of Misery,* to me at least a hundred times daily. While he encouraged me to join his angry refrain, I completely missed the irony of the line, "Remember, misery loves company."

He was right. And I learned that it is easy to find people who will join you in your anger and misery but are not interested in journeying deeper with you.

It is good to know you are not alone in those difficult moments. But living out of a wound without ever going deeper is not the best end destination. We can end up walking in circles with the wounded multitudes on the periphery of an angry status quo without any idea that there is a more generative and healing path.

That was me.

Granted, I was a young man. But even when people created space for me to go deeper, I was content walking along the angry edges, living out of my wound, and seeking out those who would validate and join me in my anger.

I remember one of my teachers, Benny Newell, who met me at Hardee's one early morning to see how I was doing. There were no forced agenda or talking points. He did not chastise me for being hurt and angry. He patiently listened and walked with me as I carried my wound, hoping I would go deeper. But I never did. All I could do was hide my burning hatred behind empty platitudes.

When those closest to us say they are "holding space" for us, I wonder how often we miss the opportunity of their generosity. How frequently do we neglect the space they give us to breathe and self-reflect? Why are we so quick to deflect and refuse an occasion to look inwardly at who we have become? When those who love us create space to search our motives and impulses manifesting from our wounds, why is it so difficult to see the gift they give us?

Question

Think about the company you keep during difficult times. How might seeking support that encourages growth and healing, rather than just sharing in misery, foster forgiveness and aid in your journey towards personal transformation?

Week 31

WOUNDED HEALERS UNITE

I READ A STORY from the Washington Post about a seventh-grader named Brody Ridder. Two years prior, he transferred to a school in Westminster, Colorado, and had difficulty fitting in and finding friends. To make matters worse, he was the target of significant bullying.

At one point, as the students received their yearbooks and ceremoniously signed each other's pages, Brody's yearbook remained largely untouched. Despite asking classmates to sign his yearbook, they refused. While everyone else had hundreds of notes from their friends, the seventh-grader had three notes, including one written to himself.

"Hope you make some more friends- Brody Ridder."

Frustrated at her son's bullying, Cassandra Ridder posted a picture of her son's heartbreaking note in a private group for school parents. She hoped her post would increase awareness of bullying and encourage parents to talk to their kids. She could not have imagined what would transpire.

But then, a remarkable change began to take shape. News of Brody's plight started to circulate, reaching the ears of older students in the school. They flocked to his classroom and filled his yearbook with hundreds of uplifting notes. Their act of kindness was not just profound but also contagious. Soon enough, Brody's classmates, too, found the courage to stand up and sign his yearbook.

One eighth-grader reflected on why she encouraged her friends to join her in signing Brody's yearbook. "No one helped me when I was [bullied]," she said, "so I wanted to be there for him." Her simple act of empathy and support sparked a chain reaction of kindness, leading to a significant shift in Brody's social standing and emotional well-being.

Her wound was the impetus for her being a healer.

This story is a lesson in how easily we wound one another but also in what we ultimately do with our wounds. We can allow our pain to become toxic and spread through our words and actions. Or, like the eighth-grader, we can use our wounds as a healing salve for others.

Richard Rohr once said, "It's all about what each of us does with the wound. If we have never walked through some kind of suffering, whether betrayal, abandonment, rejection, divorce, loss of job, struggles with sexuality, we probably will give people' head' answers. We don't touch or heal their hearts because our own have not been transformed." This quote underscores the importance of personal transformation and empathy.

This transformation is not an exercise in erasing our wounds as if they never existed. We will always carry them to one degree or another. The point is, however, to invite forgiveness and love into that painful place. This means acknowledging our pain, accepting it as part of our journey, and choosing to respond with forgiveness and love, both for ourselves and for others. This process can lead to healing, not just for ourselves, but also for those around us.

Question

Reflect on a time when your own wounds helped you connect with someone else's suffering. How did this shared experience foster healing and understanding for both of you, and what role did forgiveness play in this process?

Week 32

EMBODYING HEALING

DAY 1

Action: Identify a situation or person in your life where you struggle with forgiveness.

Reflection Question: What specific emotions or past experiences are tied to your struggle with forgiveness in this situation? How do these factors influence your reluctance to forgive?

DAY 2

Action: Reflect on what forgiveness means to you and how it differs from condoning or excusing behavior.

Reflection Question: In what ways can redefining forgiveness as a personal, internal process rather than a transactional act help you move towards healing? How does this shift in perspective affect your approach to the situation?

DAY 3

Action: Choose a specific aspect of the situation where you want to begin practicing forgiveness.

Reflection Question: How can breaking down the process of forgiveness into smaller, manageable steps make it more attainable for you? What initial actions can you take to move toward forgiveness?

DAY 4

Action: Begin the process of offering forgiveness through a tangible act, such as writing a letter (you don't have to send it), engaging in a kind gesture, or having a conversation if appropriate.

Reflection Question: How do your thoughts, emotions, and interactions change as you start practicing forgiveness? What surprises or insights have emerged from this practice so far?

DAY 5

Action: Reflect on the outcomes of your forgiveness efforts over the past few days.

Reflection Question: How has your practice of forgiveness influenced your emotional well-being and your relationship with the other person? What specific changes have you observed in your thoughts and behaviors?

DAY 6

Action: Make any necessary adjustments in your approach to forgiveness based on your reflections.

Reflection Question: What challenges or obstacles have you encountered in your forgiveness journey, and how can you overcome them? How can you integrate the lessons learned into other areas of your life?

DAY 7

Action: Plan how to integrate the practice of forgiveness into your daily life beyond this week.

Reflection Question: What specific practices or routines can you establish to ensure that forgiveness remains a central part of your daily life? How can you hold yourself accountable to maintain this focus?

WEEKLY WRAP-UP

Reflection: As you reflect on the week's experience, what have been the most significant moments of growth or transformation for you? How can you continue to build on these insights and apply them to other areas of your life and relationships?

PEACE

Week 33

An Invitation to My Divine Comedy

Jenny told me she was over a week late on her period.

Let me tell you.

When you are an almost 48-year-old man who had a vasectomy over a decade ago and who has three kids (22, 19, and 10), the last thing you want to hear are those words.

Like a gray-bearded soldier, hoping he had already fought in his last war, I marched into Fort Walgreens and stealthily purchased a box with two tests. Walking out to my car, I began laughing out loud at the hilarity of my divine comedy.

With the bathroom door secure from a potentially wandering 10-year-old, we waited for two minutes, which were twenty years.

The 99.9% accurate digital test flashed.

Pregnant.

You have likely heard the phrase *build your house upon the rock rather than the sand.* The point is that a house built upon the rock can withstand strong winds and heavy storms better than a foundation that easily washes away.

This firm foundation that centers a person and gives solid grounding has to be peace and love. Despite what storms may blow our way, the foundation of peace and love firmly grounds us, enabling us to stand firm. That is why I insist on each of us cultivating a healthy and vibrant *inner self.* When our center is peace and love, we have the resiliency to handle the most unpredictable life situations.

At that moment, I was glad I had been working on my *inner self* because this shocking development was something I never expected. After hugging

Jenny and nervously laughing, I told her I would pour every ounce of love and wisdom into our baby. It was not the path I imagined us taking at that point in our lives, but I received it with a peaceful soul.

That is the foundation we are all working to establish together.

Interestingly enough, after three subsequent pregnancy tests and a fourth from the doctor, it turned out that Jenny was *not pregnant*. The first test was a false positive. I could have told you that earlier, but I wanted you to have the same experience we had over those two days.

Question

When faced with an unexpected and potentially life-changing situation, how can cultivating inner peace and love help you navigate through it with grace and resilience?

Week 34

The Day I Turned Off the News

I QUIT WATCHING THE news fifteen years ago.

I do not remember what exactly caused me to turn it off, but as I sit here now and reflect, we were several years past 9/11. Whatever sense of humanity and community we had discovered amongst ourselves on 9/12, it had slowly devolved into partisan politics, ideological division, and the dehumanizing of the *other*. While we were ultimately accountable for what we were becoming, I noticed how the news media curated content to keep us angry and at odds, how it kept *me* angry and at odds.

These words of wisdom ring perpetually true, whether they were first written thousands of years ago, in the aftermath of 9/11, or today—that *which you gaze upon, you become.* This means that the things we focus on, whether positive or negative, profoundly influence our thoughts, feelings, and actions.

When your source is anger, you will become angry. When you feast upon hatred, you will become hateful. Or conversely, when you reside in peace, you will become peaceful. When you choose a more generative path, you become generative yourself.

You can see the pattern.

That which you invite to be your emotional center can either ravage your spiritual well-being or bring you to life. For instance, if you invite gratitude, you will find more things to be grateful for. If you invite joy, you will find more reasons to be joyful.

The same is true for how we see God. If we gaze upon a God that we believe is in short supply of mercy, limited in grace, and scarce in love, is that not what we will become ourselves? In other words, our perception of God influences our beliefs, shaping our actions and character.

Our emotional center is a potent force that can either uplift or destroy our well-being. If we choose to focus on kindness, how can we not become kinder towards ourselves and others? If our source is love, how can we not become more loving towards ourselves, other people, and our world? It's a transformative power we all possess.

Question

Does what you focus on regularly contribute to your inner peace and well-being, or does it lead to feelings of bitterness, anger, and hatred? How can shifting your focus help you cultivate a more positive life filled with kindness and love?

Week 35

THE LAST CIRCLE

THE FOLLOWING EXCERPT FROM my novel *What Can't Be Hidden* explores one character's realization that inner peace is essential for relational and communal peace.

I'm the one who admitted to being the sick system, Ochi thought. I'm the one who said I take it with me everywhere I go. I've been so preoccupied with everyone else's ills and wrongs and misgivings that I built up a wall around my heart. And if I can't even look behind that wall and change myself, how do I expect anything around me to change? If there's something toxic behind that wall, does it not flow outwardly into everything else? If there's pain behind that wall, how could it not be felt by those around me? If my anger and resentment and pride reside behind that wall, they've had to affect my relationships with those closest to me? Maybe Patrida isn't at peace because I'm not at peace. But how can anything penetrate this wall I've constructed around my heart?

"You see it this time. I know you do," Sophia called out for the last time as she hobbled toward her son.

"You know, a person can spend so much time on the other side of these circles," Ochi said, "without ever going inward, without ever having to go deeper. That's me. I thought I knew what peace was, but I had no idea."

"So true, Ochi," Sophia said. "Peace is not something a person can create or manufacture from the outside. Peace can only exist within you."

"That's what's so surprising to me, I guess," Ochi confessed. "I've spent so much of my life believing peace was something outward that we needed to strive for as a community, that if we agreed to it, then it must be true. I mean, we lived by the motto *Peace through Strength* in Patrida, yet not a single one of us knew what peace was. Isn't that crazy? We believed we were the ones living in peace, yet there you sat for all those years confined behind four, dark walls, and you were the only person in Patrida who had found it."

"And it was this peace, Ochi, that allowed me to come back to you," Sophia said, slowly kneeling next to him. "Peace is not an ideal for which we strive. When it is an ideal, it is only a word on our lips or an idea existing in our heads. But when peace resides in your heart, it becomes your lived experience. Peace becomes the way you begin to see and relate to the world. That is the key to our relationships. Relationships can only begin to heal when peace resides within each person. And a community will only begin to heal when our relationships are at peace. But for a circle to expand and include others in that peace, it must begin as the smallest of circles around one's heart."

Question

How might cultivating inner peace help you foster forgiveness towards those who have hurt you, and how can this inner transformation positively impact your relationships and community?

Week 36

GARBAGE IN, GARBAGE OUT

I HAVE BEEN PICKING up litter throughout my neighborhood and around town for about a month. Walking by myself with a trash bag in hand has given me a lot of time to think.

As I embarked on this mission to clean up litter in my neighborhood and town, I pondered its origin. It was a mix of trash that had blown out of trash cans, some from homeless encampments under bridges and in wooded areas, and a significant portion intentionally thrown on the ground by people. This realization made me question the reasons behind such actions.

While I do not fully understand why people litter, a part of me somewhat understands it. Perhaps it's a reflection of our own internal clutter, our unresolved emotions and frustrations, that we unconsciously project onto our surroundings.

How I feel inside often manifests in everything else I do. In most cases, that is the situation without painting too broad a stroke.

How we feel about ourselves affects how we feel about everything, from our relationships with our community to the care we extend to our environment. How we view ourselves ripples into our relationships, community, and even the care we extend to our environment. This interconnectedness underscores the importance of self-love in fostering a healthier, more caring world.

There is a profound wisdom that forms the foundation of a whole and fully integrated life. It involves loving God with your whole heart and loving your neighbor as yourself. This wisdom suggests that our ability to love outside of ourselves is directly related to our ability to *love ourselves*. When we do not *love ourselves*, it is nearly impossible to love others, our community, or our environment. It's a powerful concept that resonates deeply with me.

But many people, especially young people, would say it is impossible to *love yourself* when you do not even *like yourself*.

I understand.

But every strong, healthy tree that produces fruit must begin as a meager seed nurtured in soil.

In the same way, love must be cultivated within to become a person who can begin to love inside and outside yourself.

Question

How can nurturing positive thoughts about yourself cultivate inner peace and lead to more loving actions toward your community and environment?

Week 37

CRAFTING JOY

IN THIRD GRADE, WE had an Author Fair. Each student had to write a book for the competition. This story is embarrassing, and I'm unsure why I'm sharing it.

But here we go.

The teacher gave us blank paper to fold into a book. We wrote a story and drew pictures for each page.

My book was titled *The Fingernail Fink*. The title used alliteration (well done) and included the word "fink," though I misunderstood its meaning. Am I stalling in telling you the story? Yes, of course. Why? Because the premise was that the Fingernail Fink, a shadowy figure only appearing at night, broke into houses to steal...wait for it...discarded fingernails.

I know, I know. Please, don't judge me. I was only a child.

But I wish I could have seen the teacher's and judge's reactions to my masterpiece. It was weird, for sure, but I went for it. And I remember how fun it was to create.

Luckily, my creative writing improved by the time I was a freshman at Hanover College, taking English Composition. The professor gave us an assignment to find a magazine ad and write a story about it. I chose a whiskey advertisement with an ironic picture of a truck with a flat tire hauling tires in its bed. When I got the paper back, the female professor wrote that my writing made her want to, "pour [herself] a Windsor Canadian Supreme, fluff up [her] pillows, light a smoke, and relax."

Whew!

I loved writing for writing's sake. It brought me joy. However, in 2016, I wrote a blog post sharing this, "In recent years, I have become discouraged with writing. Not the content, which was always fine, but this nagging question hung over me like a heavy cloud—Why waste time writing when no one reads or pays attention?"

I believed my joy in writing depended on readership. I recognized my mistake and apologized to those who read that confession.

But that's the temptation. We can believe our work, craft, talents, and creativity are tied to who sees, likes, loves, or pays attention to it. We risk sacrificing joy and the experience of doing what we love by thinking it's only worthwhile if celebrated by the masses—whether a social media post, our work, or our creations.

The truth, and my hard-earned wisdom, is that joy lies in the creation and sharing, no matter how many people see it.

My joy in the creative process and sharing these stories with those who will read them exists whether the audience is one or many.

Question

How can cultivating a deeper appreciation for the process itself in your creative or daily activities foster inner peace, allowing the act of creation to be a source of joy independent of the outcome or external acknowledgment?

Week 38

Floral Footprints

OUR FAMILY'S LONG-AWAITED TRIP to Seattle finally materialized during Spring Break. It was a moment of serendipity, a convergence of calendars that had been four years in the making. Our initial plans were thwarted by the coronavirus outbreak in Washington state in March 2020, but in 2024, we were finally able to take that trip together.

On one of our first days, we visited Pike Place Market. You've likely seen pictures of this iconic location– thousands of bustling bodies, guys throwing fish, tourists staring at gum walls, and the most vibrant collection of flowers, fresh fruit, and vegetables. It's a bucket list place, for sure. And the food! My, oh my. Sorry, I'm getting carried away. But if you ever get the chance to visit Pike Place, do it.

As we walked the sidewalk, weaving through a maze of people, I kept my head down, looking at my feet. I caught a fascinating, yet swift, glimpse of colors between concrete sections. I thought it was interesting, but I continued walking to keep up with my family's fast and determined pace. Still looking down as I walked, I noticed the same thing repeatedly in the cracks. Finally, I stopped and examined the colors. Someone had pressed small flowers side-by-side along the entire length of the sidewalk. I smiled and wondered who had taken the time to accent this path with such a delicate touch.

It wasn't long until I found out.

Sitting cross-legged while people hurried past, a humble figure caught my eye. An older woman leaned over and meticulously placed small flowers into the sidewalk seam. Time after time, she reached into a small plastic container holding the flowers and continued the detailed process. Her actions were a testament to the power of small acts of kindness, a gentle reminder that we all can make a difference, no matter how small.

Before I left for this vacation, I had been meditating on these words– *Those who are with me gather, while those who are against me scatter.* These profoundly wise words of Jesus break down our endeavors into two fundamental categories: gathering or scattering. One is fundamentally productive, the other unproductive. This means we can use our time, energy, effort, words, resources, and endeavors to bless, heal, and do good or to curse, wound, and harm. It's a powerful reminder of our choices' impact on the world around us.

What I saw in this modest woman on the sidewalk at Pike Place Market highlighted what I had been meditating on. No matter who we are or where we find ourselves, no matter our status or position, no matter our abundance or lack, and no matter our past or present, we can consciously choose to gather over scattering. We can determine how we will bless rather than curse, heal rather than harm. We can decide to leave a trail of kindness and beauty in our wake, much like the unassuming artist with her flowers.

Question

How can consciously choosing to gather rather than scatter in your daily life cultivate inner peace, and how can incorporating more acts of kindness and beauty in your actions and words positively impact those around you?

Week 39

GESTICULATIONS, SHENANIGANS, AND THE MICRO-OFFENDED

IT'S A SCENE WE'VE all witnessed these days. My wife, like many, had pre-ordered and was doing a curbside pick-up at the grocery store. She entered the parking lot and got in one of the car lines. In her rearview mirror, she saw an angry lady in her car, yelling and gesticulating. *Gesticulating* is a fun word. Unbeknownst to my wife, the other lady was parked in an actual parking spot, waiting for one of the pick-up spots to open up.

Simple mistake.

Realizing her oversight, Jenny attempted to let the lady know she had made a mistake. But the shenanigans continued—another fun word—*shenanigans*. Instead of trying to explain her error, she just backed out and let the other customer go ahead.

But man.

We are on the edge these days, aren't we? And I'm not saying that in a humorous way. I am saying it in a sad indictment kind of way. It's no wonder there are so many people attacking and killing each other for the most inconsequential things. Our incidental actions (even our mistakes) have become life-or-death issues. We are ready to come unglued at the slightest inconvenience or micro-offense (yes, I just used *micro* to describe an *offense*. I hope it didn't micro-offend you). If there is such a thing as the death of patience and kindness, I think we're almost there.

I've been thinking a lot about this lately. I would really like to resurrect kindness rather than plan a funeral for it. I would rather draw attention to the problem and seek solutions than watch us continue this downward spiral. I would rather actively and intentionally practice kindness in my life than exist as an impulsive ball of anger ready to explode at the slightest micro-offense. Sorry, I had to.

I got a call yesterday while doing some administrative work in my office. The caller ID showed the number coming from Hollywood, California. I never pick up numbers I don't recognize. However, in the last month, I randomly met two people with Hollywood connections who wanted a copy of my first novel. I knew the call was not likely to be *the call*, but I had to pick it up, right?

So I did.

And, as expected, it was a self-publishing company trying to get me to spend money with them to publish a book. At that moment, I thought about the death of patience and kindness. I thought about the person on the other side of the call. She was doing her job, and cold-calling is a *tough job*. I decided to listen to her pitch even though I wasn't interested. I told her she had a formidable job and that I appreciated her. Her tone showed me that she was glad I treated her with dignity and respect.

I don't know. Maybe that's what it's all about. Maybe there's more to life than rushing through it to get to the next thing, our daily intermittent explosive disorders or being micro-offended about everything. Maybe, just maybe, there's more to it all.

Question

How can cultivating inner peace help you respond with patience and understanding in moments of misunderstanding, rather than reacting with frustration?

Week 40

The Pee on the Seat

WALKING INTO A UNISEX restroom at a coffee shop, I was confronted with a situation that perfectly encapsulated the theme of misunderstanding. Approaching the toilet, I noticed someone had urinated on the seat. That wasn't a problem, as I would not be sitting down. However, I faced a huge dilemma. I didn't want to wipe up a stranger's pee from the seat. But, if I walked out of the restroom and someone was waiting to go in, they would misunderstand the situation and think I was the one who caused the mess. I cleaned it up since I didn't want the coffee shop staff to clean it up and because I didn't want anyone to think I urinated all over the seat.

Here's another story.

Once again, I had a situation where someone could misunderstand me. As a modern-day hunter-gatherer, I made my way home from a Target pick-up a few evenings ago. In my subdivision, long grass islands separate the two lanes. If someone blocks the lane, you can momentarily shift between grass islands to get around the blockage. This particular evening, a big truck with blinkers (no driver) made it obvious I would have to switch lanes. Maneuvering over, I drove in the opposite lane until I reached the turn for my street. Of course, right on cue, someone pulled up to turn into the road I was traveling. They angrily stared at me, imagining I was doing it for fun or not understanding basic driving etiquette. I sheepishly made my turn without any opportunity to explain myself.

Misunderstanding is difficult. It is the foundation of our relational and societal dysfunction—how we immediately jump to conclusions about others with limited information. Rather than having a patient posture, we are quick to assume the intentions of others.

In my novel *And So By Fire*, I write about our difficulties in misunderstanding each other. Here is what I write:

> Had an autopsy been done at that moment, misunderstanding would have been the cause of death. A mere five senses had attempted to interpret and translate a complex reality. But senses ultimately fail when manipulated, and an individual's uniquely lived experience skews their perception. Considering these factors, misunderstanding was inevitable.

And then:

> With so many variables at play, all shaping one's view of the world, grace was the only countermeasure capable of neutralizing their misunderstandings. But it was a nonexistent virtue.

Question

How can cultivating inner peace help you handle minor inconveniences or misunderstandings in a way that avoids unnecessary conflict and reflects understanding and responsibility?

Week 41

LIVING THANKSGIVING

I WANT TO TALK about giving thanks—not as an event or a specific moment in time, but as a constant outflow of our lives.

I can already hear the cynics and naysayers shaming my idealism.

We live in a time when old hatreds have come back to life and old divisions have widened. Cultural narratives tell us that this is our only reality, and we must pick sides and prepare for battle. There is an ever-growing chorus among younger generations who believe that love has failed, that peace is for the weak, and that giving thanks is only for those who live in privilege.

I reject those notions.

No matter how dark or cynical our world has become, how jaded the news is that we consume, or how often they feed us the narrative that our only reality can be anger, hatred, and division, we can embody another way.

There is an ever-present reality into which we can enter where thanksgiving becomes the essence of our being and the perpetual outflow of our spirit.

Thanksgiving is so much more than an event, so much more than a sporadic, momentary act, so much more than an expression of gratitude only when something goes in our favor or when the conditions are right. Thanksgiving is an ever-flowing expression of gratitude in everything, in every moment of the day, with every breath taken, and never dependent upon our changing situation or circumstance.

Thanksgiving is our perpetual expression of gratitude for all people, all relationships, and all things.

Thanksgiving is our perpetual expression of gratitude regardless of our life situation or changing conditions.

Thanksgiving is saying, "This life is good. And I want to invite everyone to a seat at this table."

Thanksgiving responds amid chaos—Thank you, God, for your grace, mercy, love, and beauty. Let me be an extension of you everywhere I am, and with every breath I take.

Question

How can cultivating inner peace help you practice gratitude daily, making it a core part of your life rather than just a response to favorable events?

Week 42

EMBODYING PEACE

DAY 1

Action: Identify a situation or aspect of your life where you struggle to find peace.

Reflection Question: What specific thoughts, emotions, or external factors contribute to your struggle for inner peace in this situation? How do these elements impact your overall sense of tranquility?

DAY 2

Action: Reflect on what inner peace means to you and how it differs from simply avoiding conflict.

Reflection Question: In what ways can redefining inner peace as a state of mind and being, rather than just the absence of conflict, help you navigate this situation more effectively? How does this shift in perspective affect your approach to finding peace?

DAY 3

Action: Set a clear intention to cultivate inner peace in the identified situation or aspect of your life.

Reflection Question: How can breaking down the process of finding inner peace into smaller, manageable steps make it more attainable for you? What initial actions can you take to move toward a more peaceful state of mind?

DAY 4

Action: Begin practicing inner peace in the identified situation through mindful actions and attitudes.

Reflection Question: How do your thoughts, emotions, and interactions change as you start practicing inner peace? What surprises or insights have emerged from this practice so far?

DAY 5

Action: Assess and reflect on the outcomes of your efforts to cultivate inner peace.

Reflection Question: How has your practice of inner peace influenced your emotional well-being and your relationship with others? What specific changes have you observed in your thoughts, behaviors, and interactions?

DAY 6

Action: Make any necessary adjustments to your approach based on your reflections.

Reflection Question: What challenges or obstacles have you encountered in your journey towards inner peace, and how can you overcome them? How can you integrate the lessons learned into other areas of your life?

DAY 7

Action: Plan how to integrate the practice of inner peace into your daily life beyond this week.

Reflection Question: What specific practices or routines can you establish to ensure that inner peace remains a central part of your daily life? How can you hold yourself accountable to maintain this focus and measure your progress?

WEEKLY WRAP-UP

Reflection: As you reflect on the week's experience, what have been the most significant moments of growth or transformation for you? How can you continue to build on these insights and apply them to other areas of your life and relationships?

MINDFULNESS

Week 43

RECOVERING THE HOLY ORDINARY

My DAUGHTERS AND I embarked on a challenging hike, ascending 2900 feet over six miles, to reach the breathtaking Gore Lake near Frisco, Colorado. This lake, nestled in the heart of the Rocky Mountains, is a haven of tranquility and natural beauty. We had planned to stay two nights on the lake, immersing ourselves in its serenity, and then hike out. I awoke before the girls on the first morning, grabbed my small stove, and made coffee by the lake.

In the stillness, I watched the fog quietly creep over the pass and dissipate as it met the sun's first rays. Concentric circles multiplied across the water's surface from the opportunistic fish. For an hour, savoring my coffee, I watched ants moving to and fro in front of me, diligently working and moving materials twice their size.

It was one of the most beautifully ordinary moments of my life, but it felt *holy. It was* a moment of profound connection with nature and a sense of something greater than myself.

On another backpacking excursion in Alaska, the guys and I approached the top of Mount Eielson with Denali towering in the distance. No one spoke, as if we knew what to do and what the others were thinking. Along the ridgeline, we drifted apart, equidistant, to sit, stare, marvel, contemplate the beauty, and drink in the magnificence. It was another indescribably humbling, awe-inspiring, and deeply spiritual moment. There was a shared solemnity, a communal rite of the sacred and holy.

But experiencing the *holy*, a term I use to describe a profound sense of divine connection and wonder in a seemingly ordinary moment, does not require going to Colorado or Alaska. I have been with individuals who were no more awake sitting by an alpine lake or climbing a mountain than when they were sitting at work.

The truth is that the ability to open ourselves to a *sacred* moment is within our grasp. It requires nothing more than our presence and our willingness to be fully present now.

Presence permits you to turn down the volume of all distractions and be here, now.

It allows you to turn off your phone or leave it at home while you take a long walk and contemplate the beauty of the sun's rays breaking through the trees, the snow falling delicately from the sky, or the wind blowing through your hair. It is shutting down social media so you can sit quietly and observe the details, intricacies, and wonders around you. It is acknowledging that there may be troubles, but for now, you will close your eyes and listen to your heartbeat while meditating on every breath and all that is good.

Question

How can I cultivate mindfulness to find moments of peace and significance in my everyday surroundings, and what simple practices can help me appreciate these moments more deeply?

Week 44

From Panic to Perspective

I ALMOST HAD A panic attack– and I don't mean that metaphorically. It was an overwhelming mix of fear and helplessness, a moment where I felt utterly out of control. Until that point, I had never experienced anything quite like it.

My son, Will, and I decided on a whim to leave Columbus, Indiana for a spontaneous trip to the Upper Peninsula of Michigan. After a seven-hour drive, we stopped in Mackinaw City before continuing our journey to Pictured Rocks National Lakeshore. At the public beach, we were in awe of the stunning four-mile suspension bridge connecting the landmasses. We spent time skipping rocks, and eventually, Will even bravely jumped into the frigid waters of Lake Huron for a swim.

Despite the apparent enjoyment of the moment, my mind was racing with thoughts. The trip was entirely unplanned, and I couldn't help but worry about where we would sleep, what we'd do, and how everything would unfold. Even though I had brought a tent, uncertainty weighed heavily on me. As we finished dinner at a very basic pizza place, which surprisingly turned into Will's favorite topic of conversation for the next couple of days, an overwhelming feeling of uncertainty crept in, accompanied by the fear of letting Will down with what I thought would be a lackluster "boy's trip." I asked Will to wait in the car while I made a phone call.

Thankfully, my wife answered, and I expressed my feelings to her. She offered me a much-needed perspective, reminding me that every moment Will and I spend together is meaningful to him. For Will, it's not about grand plans or constant entertainment. All that matters is that he gets to share quality time with me.

And she was right.

I had unknowingly fallen into the trap of thinking I had to constantly entertain Will to ensure he had a good time. Despite all my reflections on living in the present and cherishing the small things, I had lost sight of what truly matters. No matter how simple, every activity we do together holds immense significance for Will simply because we are doing them together. It won't be about whether I planned everything perfectly or managed to keep him entertained. The memories he'll treasure the most will be the moments we share, side by side.

When I asked him, Will said that the best part of our trip was spending time together on a small, secluded beach, swimming for hours in Lake Superior. It was a powerful reminder that what we need most is not a multitude of things to keep us occupied but rather presence. It's the bond we share that will carry with them throughout their lives.

Question

In what situations do I find myself overwhelmed by expectations, and how can practicing mindfulness help me value presence over perfection?

Week 45

Mr. Monkey Brain

I RECENTLY WATCHED A fantastic four-episode documentary on Netflix called Chimp Empire. Based in the Ngogo forest of Uganda, the episodes follow two separate communities of chimpanzees that navigate complex socio-political dynamics, family issues, and territorial disputes.

Interestingly, these two communities used to exist as one large, single community. But now, they are bitter adversaries, competing for land and resources.

Jackson, a 31-year-old male, led the Central group and was the alpha leader before the split.

While I was deeply enthralled and captivated by these communities of chimps (you don't see chimps in Indiana), I was mesmerized by Jackson. The hulking behemoth was constantly studying the interpersonal relationships between others. If he didn't like who was grooming who, who was spending more time who, or who was trying to assert themselves in the group, he lost it. He would begin shrieking and huffing while running around, pulling branches, and hitting trees to assert his alpha-maleness and displeasure. In response, scared mothers grabbed their children and left the area. Everyone else shrieked and huffed to affirm his temper tantr...show of dominance.

As I watched Jackson, I was like, "Oh, that's me." No, I don't run around my house with my clothes off, pulling patio chairs around and smacking the brick of my home. But my dang monkey brain, my most primal instincts, kick in when triggered.

Believe it or not, I have a passive/avoidant communication style. My goal in dealing with those who have an aggressive communication style is to avoid or indirectly resist conflict. The problem is that I may not say anything to an aggressive person, but I let it bottle up within me. I become an ever-inflating ball with no release valve. Unfortunately, this makes me incredibly reactionary or impulsive to the slightest trigger. I become Jackson, but instead, I use sharp, unkind words in a frustrated or angry tone.

See. I told you I'm not perfect.

But I believe that acknowledging our imperfections is the first step towards growth and self-improvement.

I recently started coaching sessions to identify how I am feeling and what triggers me. I am paying more attention to my feelings and impulses and learning how to advocate for myself with aggressive communicators so that both sides win and there is a more equitable power dynamic. More importantly, I am learning that to find peace, sometimes it has to be more than just saying it, aspiring to it, or hoping it magically arrives in my heart. It takes necessary, intentional work to rewire our brains and change our hearts. This awareness reminds me of a quote from St. Francis of Assisi when he wrote, "While you are proclaiming peace with your lips, be careful to have it even more fully in your heart."

Question

What triggers my instinctual reactions, and how can practicing mindfulness help me become more aware of these impulses to respond more thoughtfully in stressful situations?

Week 46

MISSING MOMENTS

I EXPERIENCED AN UNEXPECTED emotion the other day. I was not crying or anything. It was just a deep sense of joy and gratitude.

My parents were visiting us. Will (my 11-year-old) grabbed my dad's phone and started watching videos of himself when he was little. I wasn't paying much attention as I was watching a basketball game. At one point, though, he started laughing and insisted I watch one of his videos.

Let me describe it: Will discovers a Star Wars action figure, still in its original packaging, at my parent's house, which belonged to me when I was younger.

I have to tell you, watching that video filled me up. I could see the excitement in Will's eyes and hear it in his voice. And then at the end he says, "I'll see you tomorrow, dad." The dramatic pause. And then, "I love you." Oh man, all the feels. That's a video I will be replaying a lot as I get older.

My first impulse was to write about how generative it is to look at pictures, watch videos, or even reflect on our time with those we love. While I thought that was a good idea, something else hit me as I sat down to write this. I thought about how important it is to be present and not miss opportunities as they happen.

You see, I don't ever recall seeing that video of Will. I suppose it's possible that my parents never sent it to me, but I think it is much more likely that I received it and didn't give it my full attention, quickly watching it and moving on. I wonder how many other (lesser) things I was preoccupied with at the time that I missed Will's excitement and tenderness. If I'm honest, I allow too many distractions to rob others of my full attention and presence.

And that means I miss moments or opportunities to delight in those close to me.

So, while I will continue to watch this video and be filled with joy seeing Will's excitement and tenderness, I am also resolved to be less distracted, so I don't miss moments the first time.

Question

What are some beautiful or meaningful moments you might have missed because you were distracted or preoccupied? How can practicing mindfulness help you become more aware of and cherish these fleeting experiences in your daily life?

Week 47

Unveiling Life's Boring Moments

I HAD THE OPPORTUNITY to lead a creative writing session with the fifth-graders at Will's elementary school. I wanted it to be fun and engaging with several individual exercises, so I chose descriptive writing. I had the kids think about their senses as they write. I told them to help the reader see what they see, hear what they hear, and feel what they feel.

I asked everyone to close their eyes and think about the first day of school—what did you see, hear, taste, smell, or touch? After some protested, saying they could not remember that morning, they got quiet. After a few minutes, I had them open their eyes, take a piece of paper and a pencil, and write about their experience so the reader felt like they were there.

As each student began to share, they reflected on that first morning. I felt like I was there with them. I could see it, feel it, smell it, and believe it or not, I could taste it (they had a food truck outside giving away donuts!).

This small exercise made me realize how much goodness might be around us at any given moment, but we often miss it or take it for granted unless we are actively present or prompted to pay attention to it.

As I have shared, I'm no different.

We recently planted five arborvitae trees in our backyard. Each evening, I get out the hose, sit in a chair, and water them. The first time I did it, I had my headphones in my ears. I had the sprayer in my right hand and my phone in my left hand. I scrolled and sprayed for thirty minutes, distracted from everything around me. I treated the moment as a boring task rather than a life-giving experience.

The next time I went out to spray, I intentionally left my phone behind. No headphones. Nothing. I sat down and sprayed. It was a stark contrast to the previous time. I started thinking about how much I miss these seemingly "boring" moments and how much I miss the days when I was not being stimulated every second. I thought about life before social media, gadgets in pockets, constant connection, and instant messages.

The longer I sat there, the more everything seemed to come alive, especially my trees. I can't prove it, but I swear the trees began to sing and dance as the water fell on them. Even more, they released wafts of their piney, resiny aroma. I closed my eyes and breathed in deeply. I reflected on how life-giving these boring moments can be and how I needed more of them in my life—how *we* need more of them in *our* lives.

Question

What overlooked daily activity could you approach with new curiosity, and how might practicing mindfulness transform your experience and perception of it, viewing it as an opportunity rather than a chore?

Week 48

The Road Less Taken

JENNY AND I PICKED up Will from basketball a couple of weeks ago. His school is downtown, a little less than four miles from our house. I was driving.

Now, before I go any further with this story.

Some context.

I have not worked in my hometown for 23 years and have only lived here for 25 years. My mental map of the city is less detailed and robust than that of those who live and work here. Even more, and maybe this is more of a confession, I sometimes use Google Maps to find my way around town. I know my spots and limited routes, and that's about it.

This limitation means my passengers frequently ask why I take specific routes from point A to point B. Let me say that again– My wife and kids frequently ask why I take specific routes from point A to point B. By myself, I mindlessly trek to my destinations without thinking twice. But with passengers who know the roads, side streets, and shortcuts better than me, I receive route suggestions.

On that particular day, I took a left on Central Avenue rather than a right. You don't have to know anything about Central Avenue or how it factors into the not-so-complicated matrix of me getting home to know that Jenny and Will politely questioned my choice.

"Why do you go left on Central?"

"Because it takes me to 17th and over to our neighborhood."

"It's faster to go right and take 10th," Will said. "Right, Mom?"

Will was twelve.

"Yes, 10th Street is faster, honey." Jenny didn't say "honey," but it should be in this story.

"Dad, Mom said Tenth Street is faster."

"That's what I heard," I said, but wondered how to save face with a sixth grader who would not drive for a few more years. "It's about the same amount of time, I think."

Murphy's Law.

Five longer-than-what-should-be-expected red lights later, I conceded. "I think 10th Street is probably faster."

I have reflected on this a few times since it happened. I thought about our habits and routines, the things we mindlessly do without a second thought. But then, I thought about those around us who have greater wisdom and knowledge and more experience navigating than we do. How do we receive their insights and perspectives? Do we pridefully continue the old routes? Do we self-preserve and insist we are right in our wrongness? Do we fortify the walls around our egos or take on a posture of humility to learn and grow?

Our journey to becoming our best selves is not a solitary one. It's a path that we can only tread if we trust and listen to those we love and respect. It's through this trust and openness that we can truly humble ourselves and grow.

Question

In what areas of your life are you resistant to the advice and insights of those who know better, and how can practicing mindfulness help you cultivate more humility and openness to learn and grow from their wisdom?

Week 49

WILDERNESS BEAUTY AND REFLECTION

IT WAS OUR SEVENTH day backpacking in the trailless backcountry of Denali National Park in Alaska when the early sunrise in Wolverine Creek awakened us. It would be our most significant push yet—nine miles to exit—so we needed an early start. The cloudless, blue skies welcomed our early departure from camp.

Even as we took our first steps forward that morning, we felt great satisfaction, deep refreshment, and imminent accomplishment.

Alaska could never be fully conquered, but it didn't conquer us.

And we were about to finish something very few would ever have the honor and privilege of doing.

Grizzled and chiseled, we walked through the gravelly and rocky Wolverine Creek toward Mt. Eielson. This rocky mount stood a mile above sea level and was our best and final hope of catching a glimpse of Alaska's crown jewel, Denali, which had eluded us for the previous six days.

Each labored step up the 60-degree sloped talus, which consisted of loose, softball-sized ankle busters, was aided by our trekking poles and closely accompanied by our heavy breathing. But ever so subtly, sneaking up on us westward, rising higher and higher with every foot of elevation gained, was the mighty, snow-adorned Denali in all her glory.

Our breath was taken only seconds before by strenuous activity and reduced oxygen level.

But now, our collective breath was taken by sheer majesty.

Atop the mountain was a familial union, an unbreakable bond between me, creation, and the Creator. There, a moment of singularity between heaven and earth, the two becoming miraculously one, was birthed. The invitation was a present taste of what we have always desperately longed for.

We are often content with lives that fall short of our true potential. In the absence of noise and chaos, I discovered the sacredness of solitude. In these moments, we can truly connect with ourselves and the world around us.

Question

Reflecting on your own life, what moments of solitude and connection with nature have you experienced? How can practicing mindfulness in these moments shape your sense of purpose and inner peace?

Week 50

EMPATHY IN INK

LET ME SHARE SOME hard-earned wisdom I've had on my personal journey-Changing a person's heart is rarely achieved through information.

This is a bold statement, one that I've come to understand through years of personal experience. For a decade and a half, I immersed myself in learning and translating that knowledge into blogs and books.

But over time, I discovered that instead of transforming people or fostering unity, information often had the opposite effect of dividing individuals. It became apparent that others could easily dismiss my writings by disregarding my "facts," insisting that they had their "own set of facts." The situation was disheartening because my true intention was not to engage in a battle of the facts but rather to inspire a change of heart.

In 2019, I found myself at a crossroads with my writing. The deepening ideological chasm in our country was not just a societal issue, but a personal one. The information I shared and the perspective from which I presented it were hailed by some and condemned by others. This situation was not just disheartening, it was soul-crushing. As someone who always sought to reach all audiences, even if it meant challenging some, being confined to an echo chamber was a painful reality.

I wondered if there was a different way to engage people. I reflected on how the great teachers used stories or parables to subversively disarm people and get below the surface to disengage their defensive posture. I realized that stories and anecdotes allow people to engage with difficult topics, ideas, and perspectives through flesh and blood characters. They don't require anyone to win an argument. Stories create space for nuance, perspective, and empathy because the characters are dynamic and hardly ever as dualistic as we perceive people in real life. We see their struggles. We feel their heartaches with them. We walk beside them as they wrestle through ambiguity. Through this, we can better understand how they arrive at a thought, decision, or action.

One of the most rewarding experiences of writing my first fiction book was hearing from readers who found parts of themselves in each character, even the ones they initially deemed as "villains." This revelation made me realize the potential of meaningful stories to foster empathy and understanding and to help us see ourselves in others. Perhaps, in these times of increasing division, what we truly need are more stories that inspire empathy and understanding rather than writings that further entrench our positions and create more division.

Question

Think of a story that changed your view of someone you disagreed with. How did this story help you see them differently, and how can practicing mindfulness in embracing such narratives enhance your empathy towards others?

Week 51

An Experience of Holy

One of my all-time favorite bands is Sigur Rós. You may not be familiar with this Icelandic group, but they have been creating the most exquisite, celestial, and sacred music for the past two decades. After a ten-year hiatus, they returned with their eighth album, Átta. Following the album's release, they unveiled a video for their song *Andrá*, which means *Moment*. I strongly urge you to put on your headphones (a must), watch the video, and allow yourself to be swept away by the emotional depth of this eight-minute masterpiece.

There are moments of profound connection and transcendence that exist between us, like *thin spaces*. In these thin spaces, we rise above ourselves and our circumstances, tapping into a love that resonates at the soul level. This concept of "thin spaces" is beautifully encapsulated in Sigur Rós' song *Andrá*, but it truly comes alive when you watch the video. The video shows individuals experiencing this song for the first time, and in those thin spaces, words fail, and we can't fully express the depth of the experience. These sacred moments act as a healing salve for our pain, sadness, anxiety, distress, and suffering.

Reflecting on this concept, I'm reminded of the insights I shared in my 2017 book, *Beauty in the Wreckage*:

> So while we hold together the tension of smiles and tears, the tension of joy and pain, the tension of celebration and mourning, the tension of happiness and sadness, the tension of life and death, we are still, even now, being wholly embraced, completely enveloped, unceasingly pursued, and graciously

invited into the perfect love and shalom of God through it all.

You may find that incredibly hard to fathom, but listen. Despite the wreckage around us, another reality surrounds us, immersing us in unending life and beauty. It is a reality that longs to revive our broken and wounded hearts so that they may beat again. It is a reality that washes over our blinded eyes so that we may see again. It is a reality overflowing and abundant in an ever-present completeness, wholeness, and harmony in all things. It is a reality that straightens every path, stands against and presses into the world's dark, hostile, and oppressive forces, and extends justice and righteousness for all people.

We live in a world that explodes with great artistry and creativity. It is a world that offers limitless freedom and opportunity. It is a world that flows with the greatest expressions of love and goodness. It is a world with incomparable life and beauty. We have been invited to see it with new eyes, begin living abundantly within it, and help others see and experience it. Yes, even in the wreckage, even in the worst circumstances, and even through immense and immeasurable pain, we have all been invited to enter the great embrace of heaven and earth.

Question

How can you cultivate mindfulness to become more aware of the thin spaces in your life, those moments where you feel a profound connection to something greater than yourself? How can you allow these moments to transform your perspective and bring healing to your life and others?

Week 52

THE ICEMAN EFFECT

I AM NOT TYPICALLY one to jump on bandwagons. I have a bit of a pioneer spirit and prefer discovering the next big thing rather than following what others are doing.

However, when I join a popular trend, I'm not too proud to admit it.

Enter Wim Hof, the Dutch motivational speaker known as "The Iceman," who has popularized cold plunges—submerging one's body in near-freezing waters—for numerous health benefits.

The concept of cold plunging wasn't entirely new to me. On various backpacking trips to Alaska, my friends and I would occasionally drop our packs, strip down, and dive into the glacial waters. It was shocking but also invigorating, often giving us an emotional boost to finish our trek for the day.

Recently, after researching some of Hof's health benefit claims, I bought a 100-gallon tank and set it up on my patio. It's not fancy—just black plastic. The cold nights bring the water temperature down to near freezing each morning, and I began each day by spending three minutes in the frigid water.

During those minutes, I focused on everything I was grateful for. Meditating on gratitude while enduring the cold is a real discipline, but I continued to do it every morning. The dopamine and endorphin rush from thoughts of gratitude had a profoundly positive impact on my mood.

One morning, however, I struggled to find a gracious state. My thoughts were consumed by friends and family who were hurting and suffering. I ached as I sat in the frigid waters beneath the starry morning sky. I know our sufferings do not cancel out our joys, our pain does not erase our delight, and our sadness does not diminish our gratitude. We must acknowledge them as part of this human experience and hold them all in tension.

And then I thought of you—those who may be aching on the other side of these words.

In this weekly meditation, I want to emphasize more than anything else that you are seen and loved. Even when it's difficult to imagine, know that others are with you in spirit, holding you up in prayer. We are here. We walk in solidarity with you in your painful season, carrying your burden and reminding you that there is still so much to be thankful for, even when life seems cold, dark, and hopeless at times.

Question

How can you mindfully embrace both the challenges and blessings in your life, while cultivating gratitude amid difficult circumstances?

Week 53

In All Things, Give Thanks

REFLECTING ON GRATITUDE IS a journey I embarked on many years ago, and I'd like to share a meditation I composed during that time. If you've been following my writing, you may have come across this before. However, revisiting it can bring a sense of calm and peace. So, I invite you to read, contemplate, and receive. May it be a source of tranquility as we embrace perpetual gratitude together.

Listen.

Smell.

Feel.

Close your eyes.

Take it all in and delight.

Let the wind blow at your back, and let the sun shine down on your face.

Close your eyes and listen to the conversations.

Discover the pure joy in the laughter of your children.

Celebrate that you can bathe your baby.

Find delight in the birds' songs and the leaves rustling.

Be enveloped by everything and everyone around you.

Count your blessings. It is good.

Smell the autumn fragrance.

Let the preparation of your meal be a prayer and a blessing.

Savor every bite as if it is your very first.

Feel the textures.

Let the work of your hands be praise.

Count your blessings. It is good.

Enjoy friendship as you break bread at the table.

Find life in raking the leaves, washing the dishes, and in all the seemingly mundane things.

Pause and marvel at every star brilliantly shining in the night sky.

Rejoice in every good time and bad, for it is all worth it.

Count your blessings. It is good.

Sit in the woods and notice every detail of creation.

Close your eyes and absorb every note and harmony.

Glory in every drop of your morning coffee.

Embrace the touch of another.

Join the chorus of all creation in praise.

Count your blessings.

It is good.

It is good.

It is good.

We give thanks from the depths of our souls and with every breath.

Question

How can you cultivate mindfulness to develop a deeper sense of gratitude and appreciation for the simple blessings in your life, such as the wind, sun, conversations, and everyday experiences?

Week 54

Embodying Mindfulness

DAY 1

Action: Identify a situation or area in your life where you struggle to be mindful.

Reflection Question: What specific distractions or habitual patterns of thought pull you away from being fully present in this situation? How do these factors affect your ability to practice mindfulness?

DAY 2

Action: Reflect on what mindfulness means to you and how it differs from simply being aware.

Reflection Question: In what ways can redefining mindfulness as a non-judgmental, present-moment awareness help you engage more deeply with this situation? How does this shift in perspective influence your approach?

DAY 3

Action: Set a clear intention to practice mindfulness during a specific activity, such as eating a meal or taking a walk.

Reflection Question: How can breaking down the practice of mindfulness into smaller, manageable steps make it more achievable for you? What initial actions can you take to be more mindful in this situation?

DAY 4

Action: Practice mindfulness during the chosen activity, focusing on your senses and the details around you.

Reflection Question: How do your thoughts, emotions, and interactions change as you start practicing mindfulness? What surprises or insights have emerged from this practice so far?

DAY 5

Action: Reflect on your mindfulness practice throughout the week.

Reflection Question: How has your practice of mindfulness influenced your emotional well-being and your interactions with others? What specific changes have you observed in your thoughts, behaviors, and relationships?

DAY 6

Action: Make any necessary adjustments to deepen your mindfulness practice.

Reflection Question: What challenges or obstacles have you encountered in your mindfulness practice, and how can you overcome them? How can you integrate the lessons learned into other areas of your life?

DAY 7

Action: Plan how to integrate mindfulness into your daily routine beyond this week.

Reflection Question: What specific practices or routines can you establish to ensure that mindfulness remains a central part of your daily life? How can you hold yourself accountable to maintain this focus and measure your progress?

WEEKLY WRAP-UP

Reflection: As you reflect on the week's experience, what have been the most significant moments of growth or transformation for you? How can you continue to build on these insights and apply them to other areas of your life and relationships?

TRANSFORMATION

Week 55

Unmasking the Ego

It was a significant moment when I received an unexpected email from a young woman I deeply respect. She not only appreciated my contributions to our community but also raised concerns about some careless words I had used recently. This email and the subsequent conversation it sparked brought to light a broader issue—our ego's resistance to accepting honest feedback. It made me ponder why we are so reluctant to let others speak truth into our lives.

It's common to be thin-skinned when receiving constructive criticism or healthy feedback. In a posture of self-preservation, we often react defensively to fortify our egos. We want to protect our self-image and avoid being exposed or vulnerable.

We tend to resist hearing the truth about ourselves because it can be uncomfortable and challenging. We may fear that accepting our flaws will make us appear weak or imperfect. It's as if we've built protective walls around ourselves to shield us from anything that might threaten our carefully curated image.

Our resistance to feedback can be detrimental, hindering our personal growth and damaging our relationships. When we close ourselves off from honest input, we miss out on valuable opportunities to learn and improve. It takes humility and self-awareness to acknowledge that none of us are perfect, and there's always room for growth.

So, how can we overcome this resistance and become more open to people speaking truth into our lives? It starts with the transformative power of self-reflection and a willingness to acknowledge our imperfections. Instead of viewing feedback as a personal attack, we should see it as an opportunity for growth.

Identifying those individuals we trust and respect, who can provide honest feedback with kindness, is not just important, it's crucial. Who are the people willing to ask tough questions and hold us accountable in a supportive way? These are the individuals whose input we should value most and seek out.

When faced with constructive feedback, we should strive to respond with an open heart rather than defensiveness. This process involves shedding our protective layers and recognizing that embracing the truth, even when uncomfortable, is not just a path to personal growth, but also to stronger relationships and a more fulfilling life.

In my story above, my friend's words initially stung quite a bit. But I sat with them. I eventually humbled myself and considered her perspective on my careless words. I acknowledged my mistakes, sought reconciliation, and thanked my friend for her concern. In response, I found understanding, compassion, and forgiveness.

In our complex world, we can significantly benefit from people who are open to hearing the truth and free from ego and self-preservation instincts. Let us recognize that actual growth begins with acknowledging our imperfections and embracing personal development with open hearts.

Question

How can I embrace feedback as a catalyst for personal transformation, viewing it as an opportunity to grow and improve rather than a threat to my ego?

Week 56

The Myth of This is Who I am and Who I Will Always Be

I KNOW I AM introverted. Not because Myers and Briggs told me, but because I feel it in my body and have felt it for as long as I can remember.

Don't believe my manufactured social media persona, my confident tone in writing, or my ease in public speaking. I am uncomfortable talking to people I do not know or only marginally know. I am not a chit-chatter. I frequently fail when people try to chit-chat with me. I get weird and awkward. I am almost fifty, so I have had time to accept this. Confessionally, if I see you in public, I may not come up and talk to you. Trust me. It's not you. It's me.

Don't think I am a complete psycho yet. Many years ago, I saw a person I marginally knew. After my meal, I approached this person's table and said hi. They looked at me quizzically and gave me a side-eye. They didn't know who I was.

For a poor, introverted soul like me, that was death. Finding the courage to extend myself like that, only to be embarrassed.

Woof.

Some of you who know me in real life know I am in sales. Don't worry. I do great in that profession. Ninety-nine percent of salespeople are extroverts, and my customers sincerely appreciate having someone with a different style and approach.

But I digress.

So what's the point of all this?

I love being me, and I love my unique personality and disposition. I wouldn't trade being me for anything in the world. By simply being me, I can be a blessing to others and you.

Yet, I'm also aware of the richness I miss out on in those unexpected moments, spontaneous encounters, and unplanned conversations. I could easily continue to hide in my introverted shell, using my INFJ personality as a shield or a self-fulfilling prophecy. I could resign myself to the belief that "this is who I am and who I'll always be." But the truth is, I yearn to break free from this metaphorical cocoon. I want to uncover the hidden gems in people and conversations, even if it means enduring some temporary discomfort along the way.

So, here's to embracing the awkward, stepping out of our comfort zones, and discovering the beauty in the unexpected.

Questions

How can I challenge the belief that certain aspects of my identity are unchangeable, and in doing so, open myself up to transformative growth and new experiences?

Week 57

FOUR-LETTER ASSAULT

I WAS 25 YEARS old and new on the job. My latest occupational choice had me selling ads for a newspaper. As an introvert with a background in psychology and work experience in social services, I knew this endeavor was a massive stretch for me.

One afternoon, I received a call from a business owner whose account I managed. He asked me why their daily advertisement had not been in the newspaper the previous days. I realized very quickly I had failed to schedule them. Before I could finish my meager apology, the assault began.

His word arsenal was vast and varied. He first launched the four-letter arrows to test my defenses. Realizing there would be no counter-attack, his forces pummeled me with belittling and disparaging remarks about my intellect and occupation. With my walls obliterated and my own words in stunned retreat, he cut me down, screaming f-bomb after f-bomb before slamming the phone down.

My legs were pallbearers carrying my lifeless body out of my cubicle to my place of rest (the restroom), where I closed the stall door and began to cry.

On that day, I learned firsthand how deeply words penetrate.

And in our tenuous, divided, and fragile country, we need to rethink how we speak to each other.

The words we casually and carelessly express each day have profound power and impact on every bullied and harassed person. Our words may cause a person to doubt their worth and value. And for a person who has been verbally torn apart their entire life and can't take another hostile and demeaning word, what we speak into existence can destroy them. What we say and how we say it can push someone contemplating suicide over the edge.

The truth is that we never fully understand what a person is dealing with on the inside. That is why we should be slow to speak and thoughtful in what we say to others.

This miraculous vibrating air that manifests into exquisite expression can either be a weapon or a healing salve. It contains the potential to destroy or restore, curse or bless, and divide or bring together. Our voices can burn down mighty forests or join the heavenly refrain of all creation.

From the abundance of our hearts, so flow our words.

Question

How can I transform my communication habits to ensure that my words contribute to building and healing relationships rather than breaking them down?

Week 58

THE CENTER OF
INATTENTION

SOME OF MY MOST formative experiences happened when I was 25 years old.

Last week, I shared the story about getting verbally assaulted by one of my advertising accounts and how those dehumanizing words wounded me. While working at the same job, and likely within months of that encounter, my boss asked me to go to a Chamber of Commerce cookout in a neighboring county. She believed this would be an excellent way to make contacts and increase business.

Well, it is... if extroversion is your thing.

Unfortunately, it isn't my thing as an introvert. Being an introverted salesperson is like being a snow leopard. You know they exist, but you rarely see one in the wild. But for the record, I am in my 25th year of sales. So introverts *can* sell. We just do it differently.

But I digress.

I showed up at the Chamber of Commerce cookout and stood by a chair at an empty table. Since I did not know anyone, I hoped someone would talk to me. No one did. To make it worse, this was before smartphones and social media. I couldn't even pretend to be chatting with someone on my phone. I stood alone like a stooge with people talking and laughing around me.

I ensured I was the first in line when the buffet line opened. I didn't only want to be doing something else other than standing alone. I wanted to sit at a table first and force people to sit at my table when the other tables filled up. I also figured that the table most likely to fill up first was the one in the center. So that's where I sat. In the center.

Person after person went through the line, each finding a seat at a surrounding table. One by one, the tables around me filled up. Not only was I the lone person at my table, but I had finished eating and sat like a lonely imbecile for the next hour.

It was my worst nightmare.

I always wondered why someone didn't notice I was by myself and invite me to their table. Was it not evident to the 150 people sitting around me that I had no one at all, that I was awkwardly, painfully alone? Because if someone had invited me to their table, I would have jumped at the opportunity.

Question

Reflecting on a time when you noticed someone in need but did not act, what held you back? How can you transform this hesitation into compassionate action in the future?

Week 59

THE BUTT HURT CUSTOMER

MY MOTHER-IN-LAW WAS WITH some friends at a local mom-and-pop restaurant for breakfast. As with many businesses post-pandemic, the restaurant was grappling with a severe shortage of staff. In the midst of a tight labor market, some employees had quit while others were unable to come in due to illness. The one or two people who were working were valiantly trying to manage everything, but it was an uphill battle.

Customers were frustrated by the restaurant's lack of service and the time it took to prepare food. The tables were dirty, and there were few places to sit.

The ladies, understanding the workers' plight and feeling their struggle, made a conscious choice. Instead of walking away, venting their frustration, or simply observing her battle to keep up, they decided to lend a hand. And that's exactly what they did.

This story is very instructive.

We can choose how we react and respond to situations that are not ideal. There is no question that many of us have been shaped by what we believe we are entitled to. We live in an 'expectation culture, where we expect service to be a certain way. We expect that we are always right as the customer. And we expect that our goods and services need to meet our standards. If any of those expectations are unmet (for whatever reason), we let people know what we believe we are entitled to.

It's a realization that hits close to home. I witness this entitlement culture in action every day, and I'm not exempt from it either.

I took my daughter to a restaurant a few months ago. We placed our order to-go, and the young lady informed me of the amount I owed. I wanted to pay with my gift card on the restaurant's app, but it only displayed my balance. It didn't have a feature for them to scan it or input the numbers. I asked the young lady if she could access my account through her system, to which she replied negatively. In my frustration, I muttered something derogatory about the restaurant. Not only did the young lady overhear me, but so did my embarrassed daughter. I deeply, deeply regret my reaction at that moment.

Not a good dad moment.

Not a good human being moment.

I have a feeling our expectations in the coming weeks, months, and maybe years will be significantly disrupted. What we cultivate and nourish within ourselves will determine how we respond to these changing circumstances.

Reflecting on my own experience, I've come to realize that I would much rather be a servant, helping out by cleaning off tables, than an entitled customer who can't even pay with a gift card. This realization has been a turning point for me, prompting me to strive for more empathy and understanding in my interactions with others.

Question

How can I transform my expectations and reactions in challenging situations to respond with empathy and constructive actions instead of complaints?

Week 60

The Monday That Wasn't

I walked into an office to schedule an appointment with one of my business accounts. The lady managing the appointments called for me to approach her desk. I greeted her and asked if they had any availability.

"You know better than this," she said. I didn't respond as I was attempting to ascertain her tone. She was wearing a mask that covered her mouth, which made it impossible to see if she was smiling. I raised my eyebrows and opened my eyes wide, awaiting the punchline.

"You have been doing this long enough that you know you are *not* to come in here and bother us on Mondays," she snapped loudly, continuing to huff in exasperation, staring at me in disdain. Still speechless and utterly perplexed, I stood stunned at being talked to so poorly.

Before I could make sense of her wild diatribe, her colleague leaned over and said, "Sherry (not her real name), today is Thursday, not Monday."

"Well, it's my Monday," she bellowed.

I went to a restaurant with my wife and son. As the waitress brought out our appetizer, the sauce fell from her tray, hit the ground, and splashed on the pants of a well-dressed older gentleman.

I held my breath and thought *this could go one of two ways.*

The waitress scrambled and apologized profusely. She was on her hands and knees wiping up the floor and offering to dry clean the gentleman's clothes.

Both the man and his wife replied, "It's just clothes. The sauce will come out. Don't worry about it. It was an accident."

Later that night, ten-year-old Will asked us if most people respond like the gracious older couple.

I immediately thought of my encounter with Sherry.

We have all been there, though. I have likely been more of a Sherry than the older couple. When I am not at peace within myself, I am not at peace with others. I react outwardly with what I have been feeding and nurturing inwardly. I verbalize what is in my heart.

An ancient proverb states, "Out of the abundance of the heart, the mouth speaks." Another proverb adds, "There are those who speak rashly, like the piercing of a sword, but the tongue of the wise brings healing."

What we cultivate within our hearts manifests in our words. Those words have an impact and have consequences for how they may wound or heal another.

Question

Reflect on a time when your words hurt someone. How did your inner state contribute to this reaction, and what steps can you take to cultivate a more peaceful and mindful inner self to transform your responses in the future?

Week 61

LITTLE REBELLIONS

I RECENTLY LOST MY job due to a salesforce reduction. It wasn't unexpected, but don't worry—I got a new one.

I want to reflect on how my routine abruptly changed during unemployment and share something I noticed in those early days.

With this newfound time on my hands, I began taking Will to school each morning and picking him up each afternoon. The car line is a story itself, filled with many interesting lessons and revelations, not just in strategy but in psychology. But that's a topic for another day. I would typically arrive an hour early to avoid the mass onslaught and mania of afternoon car pickup. I would read, write, catch up with people by phone, and work on projects. It was a great way to find some solitude and be productive while waiting.

Much of the time, I would stare out the windows of the car and think. I watched people walk, squirrels scurry up trees, and cars drive by. I began to notice something interesting- they were the same people every day. One of the drivers was a waiter at a restaurant I occasionally visit. Like clockwork, at 1:47 PM, he would pass by, no doubt needing to be somewhere by 2 PM.

Then, I started thinking about myself and my routine. Even though I had lost my job and my previous routine, here I was—like clockwork—sitting in the car line every day at 1:30 PM. Oh, how quickly I had become a slave to my new routine in just a few weeks. The predictability of my schedule and the comfort of my routine began to feel like a very seductive trap. While I have appreciated (and needed) a new rhythm and routine for my sanity, I was sensitive about becoming a character from *The Truman Show* or *Stranger than Fiction*.

This realization prompted a small but significant shift in my behavior. I decided to break from the norm instead of parking and waiting. I parked my car a few blocks away and walked the rest of the way to Will's school. On my way, I took time to snap some photos. While the fresh air and beauty were gifts, the best surprise was Will asking to walk downtown rather than immediately get in the car and go home.

It felt like a small act of rebellion, a leap into spontaneity and the unexpected. I may be overly dramatic. Maybe I am. But think about your routines and how you go from Point A to Point B daily. Think about how predictable it is that you will be at the same spots at certain times on certain days. Now, consider how refreshing it would be to break out of that routine just once and do something new, exciting, and different.

Question

How can breaking away from my daily routine, even in small ways, lead to new discoveries and perspectives that contribute to my personal transformation and growth?

Week 62

A Tale of Valentine's Day at White Castle

My wife suggested that we go to White Castle for Valentine's Day. I couldn't help but suspect that this clever idea was influenced by our twelve-year-old son's love for their little square hamburgers, onion chips, and the soda machine that allows him to create his own unique concoctions. The anticipation of this unconventional Valentine's Day was palpable.

Knowing that White Castle rolls out the figurative red carpet on the day of love and would likely be busy, I went online to make a reservation. To my surprise and chagrin, there wasn't a single spot available. Not to be discouraged, we made the 60-second trek from our house to do carryout. We knew it wouldn't have the same sense of romance, but at least we would be content after having our collective mindset on the WC.

We walked in together, and a hostess greeted us. She asked if we had a reservation. We explained that we tried to get one, but all the times were taken. To our surprise, there were tables they held for walk-ins! Our smiling hostess took us to our table with a red table covering, Valentine's Day menus, and a centerpiece with a candle. The atmosphere was warm and inviting, and I couldn't help but feel a sense of excitement. I could go on about the decor and ambiance, but I want to share the most memorable thing of the evening— the workers.

Of course, it is noteworthy that they would not let us do anything. Two or three workers, acting as waiters and waitresses, retrieved condiments and filled our drinks. They regularly checked on us. Okay, yeah, just like a fancy restaurant. But listen. I have never seen that much joy on the faces of fast-food workers. They were not just doing their jobs, they delighted in what they were doing. You could tell that it genuinely was their pleasure to serve.

This observation deeply affected me and made me wonder—what was it about this special event that caused the employees to be so happy and exude such joy? Was it the sense of community, the shared experience of celebrating love? Or was it the act of giving, of serving others with a smile? What are we not experiencing, creating, or tapping into daily that could elicit the same sense of fulfillment and enthusiasm in our everyday interactions?

Perhaps joy is found in the spirit of giving, in the act of selflessly providing for others. It could be rooted in the communal joy of shared experiences, in the feeling of togetherness and connection that comes from sharing a meal. It could be in breaking our routines, transforming an ordinary day into something memorable. This experience highlights the importance of creating and cultivating moments that bring out the best in us and of encouraging a culture where joy and enthusiasm are not just reserved for special occasions but are a part of the fabric of our daily lives.

Question

How can I intentionally create moments in my daily life that bring out joy, connection, and fulfillment for myself and those around me, fostering a spirit of transformation and positive change?

Week 63

THE GATHERING QUESTION

I RECEIVED AN INVITATION to a tiny gathering recently from an acquaintance. I didn't know who would be there or even how many people were supposed to attend. Despite this uncertainty, I agreed to go because I realized I don't get out as much as I should. Although I live in Columbus, I haven't worked here for the last fourteen years, and as a result, I don't know nearly as many people in town as I should for someone who has lived here for 25 years.

Upon arriving, I walked into the room and took the opportunity to get to know my acquaintance a bit better. Interestingly, she and I were friends on social media, yet we had never officially conversed. I took a seat and eagerly awaited the arrival of the other guests. When the door finally opened, three subsequent people walked in and immediately got wide-eyed, each saying, "Brandon!" I could tell their reactions stemmed from the shock of seeing me in person, but I have to tell you... it was a fantastic feeling.

Here's why.

These people are from different parts and times of my life, making the experience surreal. I had no idea they all knew each other. It was like a scene from one of my favorite movies, *Big Fish*. In this poignant scene, Will Bloom shares a story with his father, Edward Bloom, on his deathbed. In this tale, Will describes carrying his father to a river, imagining a reunion with friends from Edward's fantastical tales. As Will shares this final, imagined journey, the vivid presence of characters from Edward's stories symbolizes the fulfillment of Edward's wish, creating a deeply moving farewell.

I'll be honest, even though I have watched this movie a dozen or more times, this scene always brings tears to my eyes.

Attending this small gathering gave me the same feeling. There was something beautiful about being around these people from my past and present, all together at the same time while I was still alive. As I sat there surrounded by these unexpected but familiar faces, I couldn't help but feel a profound sense of gratitude. At that moment, I realized that we often don't get to experience the joy of being surrounded by all the people who have touched our lives until we're no longer there to witness it. Or, another way, we usually don't realize how much we're loved and how connected we are until it's too late to see it ourselves.

I wonder how we can change that.

Question

How can I actively create opportunities for meaningful gatherings and connections with the important people in my life now, fostering a sense of community and belonging that enhances our shared journey of transformation?

Week 64

Embodying
Transformation

DAY 1

Action: Identify a situation or relationship where your ego is at play and causing resistance or defensiveness.

Reflection Question: What specific patterns, beliefs, or experiences have led you to recognize the need for transformation in this area? How do these factors affect your current state and your desire for change?

DAY 2

Action: Reflect on what transformation means to you and how it differs from simple change.

Reflection Question: In what ways does viewing transformation as a holistic and profound shift, rather than a surface-level change, influence your commitment to this process? How does this understanding shape your expectations and actions?

DAY 3

Action: Choose a specific aspect of the area you identified where you want to begin the transformation process.

Reflection Question: How can breaking down the transformation process into smaller, manageable steps make it more achievable for you? What initial actions can you take to initiate transformation in this specific aspect?

DAY 4

Action: Begin applying your understanding of transformation to this area.

Reflection Question: How do your thoughts, emotions, and behaviors change as you start engaging in the transformation process? What surprises or insights have emerged from this practice so far?

DAY 5

Action: Assess and reflect on the outcomes of practicing transformation in this area.

Reflection Question: How has your practice of transformation influenced your overall sense of self and your interactions with others? What specific changes have you observed in your mindset, behaviors, and relationships?

DAY 6

Action: Reflect on areas where your ego still causes resistance and make necessary adjustments to remain open to personal growth.

Reflection Question: What challenges or obstacles have you encountered in your transformation journey, and how can you overcome them? How can you integrate the lessons learned into other areas of your life to support ongoing growth?

DAY 7

Action: Plan how you will continue to invite humility and openness into your daily life, especially in challenging situations.

Reflection Question: What specific practices or routines can you establish to ensure that transformation remains a central part of your daily life? How can you hold yourself accountable to maintain this focus and measure your progress over time?

WEEKLY WRAP-UP

Reflection: As you reflect on the week's experience, what have been the most significant moments of growth or transformation for you? How can you continue to build on these insights and apply them to other areas of your life and relationships to support ongoing personal evolution?

COMMUNITY

Week 65

A Pandemic, Wire Monkey, and a Procession of Angels

THE INCALCULABLE TOLL OF the pandemic was its impact on our mental health.

We do not have to agree whether every decision to respond to the virus was correct. But we can all agree that countless adults and children alike emotionally suffered as a consequence. We worked and schooled virtually for two years. We stayed in our homes away from our neighbors and social functions. We were quarantined in isolation and conditioned to fear being around others. And through all this, we were removed from something essential to our well-being—*community*.

In our isolation, we missed the hug of a friend, the pat on the back from the teacher, visiting our elderly neighbors, and social get-togethers after work.

In our isolation, we missed a kind glance of affirmation, a fist bump when accomplishing a task, and an encouraging word when we needed it the most.

In our isolation, we missed sharing our pains and struggles, crying in the arms of our friends, and being carried by our loved ones when we were at our lowest.

In the 1960s, social psychologist Harry Harlow discovered how isolation produced adverse behaviors in infant monkeys. Taking them from their mothers and isolating them in cages, he observed that they began to stare blankly, circle their cages aimlessly, and engage in self-harm. In a subsequent study, he introduced the choice of a wire "mother" with food or a terry cloth "mother" with no food. The infant monkeys chose the touch of another over sustenance.

We are much the same. When isolated, lost, or alone, we desperately desire the touch (or the words) of our loved ones, our people, our community, our tribe—not just to comfort us but to remind us of who we are and that we matter.

Rabbi Joshua ben Levi said in the 3rd Century, "A procession of angels pass before *each person*, and the heralds go before them, saying, 'Make way for the image of God!'"

I love the imagery he paints of those who stand before *each person*, declaring their divinity and reminding them that they are sacred and wholly loved.

In the aftermath of social isolation, how much more do we need to stand before our loved ones and remind them who they are?

Question

How can you actively reach out to someone in your community who may be feeling isolated or disconnected, and what impact might your words of affirmation have on their well-being and sense of belonging?

Week 66

PEOPLE LIKE YOU

THIS POST IS NOT political. It is a piece about how we treat each other.

About twenty-five years ago, a friend and I believed we should start an organization called *Taking Back America*. We intended to fuse faith and politics into a positive, mobilizing force. We were planning an event with some nationally recognized political speakers and faith-based musical artists.

With a few political speakers already committed, I contacted a particular artist management company to line up a musician we loved. I spoke to several people at this company and told them what we were doing and why we were doing it. I sent them our information. They said they would get back to me within a couple of weeks.

But they never did.

Frustrated, as this was the last piece of the puzzle needed to begin promoting the event, I called the agency back to find out what was taking so long. My contact transferred me directly to the agency director.

The director told me he did not believe the musician agreed with what we were doing or how we were doing it. Perplexed, I continued to press him because I could not understand what he was saying. I could not imagine a way to fix our country other than to bring faith and politics together. Even more, I could not imagine why anyone would disagree with our initiative.

However, the director continued to restate the same mantra without explanation- *faith and politics do not belong together*.

He was frustrated at my lack of understanding and continued questioning. But I was curious and earnestly seeking another perspective I had never considered. To my dismay, he refused to go beyond the safety of his one-liner and dialogue with me.

Frustrated at my lack of understanding of a position that seemed so self-evident to him, he went in for the kill.

"People like you will never get it," he yelled.

I hung up.

The director only saw me as a stereotype, a caricature. To him, I could not learn anything new, consider another perspective, or even change my mind. He did not know that I *was a* young man eager to learn. I wanted to engage with perspectives I had never previously considered. I desired opportunities with people different from me who could help me grow and expand my thinking.

Unfortunately, it didn't happen that day.

Question

Reflect on a time when you dismissed someone's perspective. How can you approach future conversations with a more open mind to foster mutual understanding and community growth?

Week 67

REMOVING THE SCARLET LETTER

I AM NOT THE same person I was in my twenties or thirties—not even the same person I was last year. From year to year, week to week, and day to day, I am constantly changing. The more I learn about myself, the more resolved I am to change—to become the best version of myself possible in this lifetime, to be more loving, patient, gracious, and kind.

However, I'm aware that I'm still more of *who I don't want to be* than *who I want to be.* Many of you have known me somewhere along that timeline. You've seen my failures, misgivings, pride, arrogance, insensitivity, and how I've hurt people with my words or actions. I may have even hurt you. So thank you for this reading anyway. Even as I write these weekly meditations, I hope you understand that I do it humbly. I recognize these words are written for me just as much as I write them for all of you.

But I think about all of this a lot.

People often hold onto an image of me from the past without affording me the grace or opportunity to change in the present. But we do this all the time—we relegate people to wear the proverbial Scarlet Letter without giving them the space, patience, grace, and mercy to change from who they used to be into a new conception of themselves—a self that is growing and transforming for the better.

I met a woman addicted to meth about fifteen years ago. I remember talking and praying with her several times while she was high. After a few weeks, I never saw her again. There were people in her life who had negative images and impressions of her during that time. Even though those images were justified, I wonder how many of those people believed she might change for the better. I wonder how many of them wrote her off instead of giving her the grace to change for the better. It's impossible to know. However, a couple of years later, she and I again crossed paths. She was clean then, and she's still clean today.

While not condoning others' bad behavior, we should avoid believing they are incapable of change or writing them off as lost causes. Everyone is a work-in-progress, constantly carrying the tension of their two realities within them. We should afford people the space, patience, grace, and mercy to change, just like we hope to receive ourselves.

Question

How can I actively support and encourage others in their journey of transformation, understanding that we are all continuously growing and not solely defined by our past?

Week 68

THE GRAY ZONE

MY DAD TOLD ME as a teenager, "This is our first time at parenting."

What he meant by the statement was that he and my mom were learning in real-time how to parent their firstborn. Being a narrow-minded young man, the idea that my parents were making it up on the fly was mind-blowing. That one cataclysmic line jolted me and forced me to consider life from their perspective.

Twenty-five years later, I was the parent of two teenagers myself.

I remember sharing with my wife how much more challenging it is to parent as kids get older. I longed for the "easy" days of parenting little children when everything was binary- a simple yes or no.

Do this.

Don't do that.

Stop bugging your sister.

Eat your food.

Don't make that face.

But as our kids got older, we constantly weighed and evaluated every decision with a million considerations. It quickly became apparent that there were no "right" answers. Nothing was black and white. We had entered the parenting gray zone.

How much independence do we give them?

Do we let them make a mistake and learn?

At what point do we intervene?

Do we tell them that we know because we read their messages?

Will this break the trust they have in us?

My mind returned to when I was a teenager, and I thought about my parents again. There was no way I could have fully understood every factor they considered with every decision. While my dad's words helped me better understand the complexities of parenting and develop a sense of empathy, it was only one step. I could only fully appreciate their perspective once I had experienced parenting myself.

I suppose that's why Jesus said, "I pass judgment on no one," because he understood that we are always limited in our perspective. We cannot fully appreciate another's life experience. We don't know what they have been through, and we don't know what factors influence their thinking or life decisions.

However, something beautiful begins to happen when we humbly enter another's story—our perspective broadens. Through conversations, relationships, and life experiences, we evolve beyond judgment into understanding and empathy. And it is from this fertile foundation that grace, mercy, and compassion toward others begin to grow.

Question

How can I cultivate empathy and understanding towards others' life experiences, and how might this shift from judgment to compassion positively impact my community?

Week 69

THE INSISTENT NEIGHBOR

IT WAS A SUMMER scorcher. I was mowing my lawn and racing to finish it. As I dumped the last bag of grass and prepared to clean up around the house, I felt like someone was staring at me. I subtly looked over my shoulder and saw my neighbor standing in his driveway with his hands on his hips and staring at me.

I went about my business as if I did not see him. But as I continued to clean up, it became apparent he was still staring. So I looked at him and politely waved without taking off my headphones or breaking my pace. He politely waved back.

But he kept staring.

Feeling uncomfortable, I stopped the blower and removed my headphones.

"Hey, how's it going?"

"Good! Why don't you come over and get in the lake to cool down?"

"Nah, that's ok. I need to finish up here."

Undeterred by my refusal, he tried again. "I absolutely insist. Come over, and we'll jump in the lake and talk for a while."

"You know, I really don't like to get in lakes (I am weird like that), but I sure appreciate the offer!"

"Well, I won't stop asking until you come over."

I humbly submitted. *I was going to cross that street and get in that lake.* His insistence overpowered my excuses for not finishing cleaning up around my house.

I walked behind his house and waded into the cool water with my clothes on. It felt terrific. Before long, my neighbor came out of his home, smiling from ear to ear with a beverage in each hand. He shared one with me as he got in the water. We talked, cooled down for the next hour, and watched the sunset paint the evening sky.

It was good. And I will never forget it.

It wasn't anything he said that opened my eyes or changed my perspective. His simple insistence was to stop the hundred-mile-an-hour rat race and enjoy the moment, the conversation, and what was around me.

Thanks to my neighbor, that day in the lake taught me a profound life lesson—sometimes, you just have to stop, breathe, and enjoy the present moment.

Question

How can you encourage yourself and others in your community to pause, connect, and appreciate the present moment amidst the busyness of daily life?

Week 70

Unlikely Conversations

As I stepped into the Uber, a stranger at the wheel, I found myself in a familiar dilemma. Should I immerse myself in the digital world, my phone a tempting escape, or should I take a leap into the unknown and engage in a conversation with this unfamiliar driver?

At that moment, my phone held undeniable allure. However, driven by a commitment to personal development, I've been challenging myself to step outside my comfort zone and embrace interactions with strangers. This airport-bound journey presented the perfect opportunity.

Our conversation, though light-hearted, revealed a man with a wealth of life experiences. A retiree from Ft. Wayne, Indiana, he had spent a quarter-century working in Asia, and was now raising his grandson in Florida. As we neared the airport, he shared his encounters with other passengers, and I couldn't help but comment, "I imagine this driving job has renewed your faith in humanity." His response was a poignant reminder of the media's tendency to focus on the negative, and his own discovery of countless instances of human kindness and delightful conversations.

Reflecting on that moment in the Uber, I'm grateful I chose to engage with our driver instead of burying myself in my phone. People are a treasure trove of stories and experiences, waiting to be shared and heard. The richness of a real conversation far surpasses the fleeting satisfaction of scrolling through a digital feed. It's easy to be consumed by the digital world, I understand that. But the real connections we make and the stories we share are what truly enrich our lives. These unexpected encounters can brighten our days, challenge our perspectives, and deepen our understanding of the world.

In a world where we're often encouraged to isolate ourselves in comfort and familiarity, engaging with a stranger was a powerful reminder. It was a lesson in the importance of not just passing through the world but truly being present in it and open to its stories, lessons, and perspectives. It reminded me of the depth and breadth of human experience, and the richness that comes from embracing it.

Question

How can I actively seek out and embrace opportunities to engage with people I don't know, and what potential impact could these conversations have on my perspective and the broader community?

Week 71

STRANGER ENCOUNTERS

I HAVE HAD SEVERAL strangers reach out to me over the last couple of months. And no, not the typical onslaught of incessant and nonstop phone calls and emails I get daily from companies trying to sell me marketing packages and national television appearances for my books. Side note: Despite blocking, reporting as spam, and deleting the phone numbers, it is incredible how many different numbers these spammers from the same companies can access! So, I only answer my phone if the call is from someone in my contacts.

Even more, I have become hesitant with people when they DM me on social media or email me. I have built up some necessary boundaries over the years to protect myself. I too easily say yes to people when I get requests. And I can extend myself to my detriment. So, I am extraordinarily cautious when I get messages from strangers wanting to meet in person or virtually.

However, I have had some time on my hands over the last few months, which has made me more willing to extend myself without sacrificing my well-being. Really quick, I am not advocating that anyone meet up with strangers. I did my due diligence by checking their connections and social media accounts. I felt comfortable that I wasn't going to be robbed at gunpoint or scammed.

But I digress.

I ended up meeting with three different people. And I am better for extending myself. One guy wanted to talk about my writing and how he was processing it and working through some things in his past. Another guy wanted to find out how he might write a book. While my meager offering about writing and books was anything but exciting, his story of running across the United States to raise money and awareness for veterans and suicide deeply moved me. His story was so compelling it nearly brought me to tears. And lastly, I talked to another guy who has a passion for the Church and rediscovering its identity and purpose in the world. As someone who has been hanging on the fringes of the Church for a while, I have been inspired by his spirit and unwavering commitment as we have continued to talk multiple times.

These conversations yielded more lessons in personal growth and how unexpected encounters can expand our perspectives and honor the intrinsic value of human connection. I know you've heard that from me many times. So, instead, I want to conclude by focusing on the hope these unexpected encounters have given me. Like my Uber driver last week, I, too, am uncovering a profound truth—*most people are very good and doing amazing things in this world.* But many times, we have to extend ourselves to realize it.

Question

In what ways have my boundaries protected me, and how might they be limiting my potential for growth and meaningful connections with others in my community?

Week 72

THRIVING IN OUR ANTARCTICA

MY FAVORITE STORY IS that of Ernest Shackleton and his expedition to Antarctica in the early 1900s.

Shackleton and his crew desired to be the first to reach the southernmost continent. But, as the autumn months passed and temperatures plummeted, his ship froze in the sea and was later crushed between ice floes, forcing him and his crew to live on the ice for two years. Their only hope of escape was to use the wooden rescue boats to cross the ocean once the waters were navigable.

Just miles short of Antarctica in mid-winter, Shackleton recalls the great irony of their situation:

> The disappearance of the sun is apt to be a depressing event in the polar regions, where the long months of darkness involve mental as well as physical strain. But the [crew] refused to abandon their customary cheerfulness, and a concert in the evening made the Ritz a scene of noisy merriment, in strange contrast with the cold, silent world that lay outside.

Despite harsh subzero temperatures, floating in dark oceanic loneliness, the crew found a way to cultivate joy amongst themselves. That does not mean every crew member was joyful every second of the two years stranded on the ice. They weren't. But they worked together, carried one another, and encouraged each other so that no man ever gave up. The community they built upon the ice sustained them. And miraculously, not a single man died during those two years stranded.

This story does not only depict individual resilience and the human will to survive. It is a story of how a community can work together, not just to exist in difficult times but to thrive. Not just for individuals to live for themselves but to notice their brother struggling and help them. Not just to live in a survival-of-the-fittest mindset but to thrive in mutual care and cooperation. Not just to wallow in pain and misery through difficult situations but to collectively cultivate joy and noisy merriment for the benefit of all.

I wonder if the same can be true for us.

Despite the darkness and seeming isolation we find ourselves in, can we take what we have been individually cultivating within (kindness, peace, and love) and share it with others? Is it possible to become a community that mutually encourages and sustains one another so that all may not just exist but thrive?

Question

Consider your community, whether it be your family, neighborhood, small group, online community, support group, or book club. How can you contribute to fostering a spirit of mutual care and cooperation so that everyone in your community not only exists but thrives?

Week 73

THE MUFFIN MAN

WE TOOK DAY-OLD PASTRIES to the local homeless shelter every Saturday morning for almost six months. My sister, who worked at a local coffee shop, brought the leftovers from the previous night so the residents would have pastries for breakfast. She would drop them off some weeks, and other weeks, I made the drop. But each time, the staff passed along their appreciation for the kind gesture.

Taking pastries to a local homeless shelter was my first attempt at breaking out of a comfortable lifestyle to which I had grown accustomed. This was a massive step for me in growing as a person. However, I was about to learn another profound lesson about people and relationships that would stretch me even more.

One Saturday morning, I arrived with a new bag of tasty treats and knocked on the door. Mary greeted me with a big smile. As one of the shelter workers, she had always been good to us when we stopped by. Mary invited me in as I handed her the bag. We briefly chatted before I said I should be on my way. As I turned and began to walk away, Mary whispered something I will remember for the rest of my life.

She said, "All the people come down to the kitchen on Saturday mornings and get a muffin. They ask where the muffins come from. I tell them that the people from the church drop them off. And they say, 'Well, tell the people from the church thank you.'"

Then she hit me upside the head with the real truth.

"The muffins are great, Brandon. But you don't know the people. You aren't sitting down with them and talking and getting to know their names. You don't know them as people. You are just dropping off muffins."

Her words were gentle, but they were daggers.

The sad reality was that I was much more comfortable with non-personal gestures and kindness than getting to know people different than me. It was easier for me to be charitable than to hang out with the "homeless." That was the flaw in my thinking. Charity was fine, but it kept me from growing and experiencing the richness of diverse relationships.

From that day forward, we brought the pastries and stayed. We sat with each other at the table. We talked. We grew. We realized muffins were best eaten together. We also developed friendships because of Mary and her words of wisdom.

Question

How can I move beyond simply performing good deeds and work towards creating meaningful connections with those I aim to help, thereby fostering deeper relationships and understanding?

Week 74

A Canned Food Extravaganza

We invited twenty or so of our closest friends to our house many years ago. We did not tell anyone what we were planning. Once everyone arrived, we gathered in our kitchen. I formed five teams and gave them the instructions.

"My wife and I are going to stay with all of your young kids," I announced. I know what you are thinking at this point. You imagine that Jenny and I sent these couples off on a date while we watched their little ones. While I appreciate you thinking of us as servants, that is not what we instructed them to do. "Your team has one hour to collect as many canned food items as possible. The only rule is that you cannot use your own money. Everything else within the constraints of the law is permissible."

They were not helping Jenny and me store up for the winter. We wanted to find a quick, impactful way to support our local food pantry before the holidays.

As the hour ended, we greeted the teams outside. While each team had a different strategy, their results were staggering. One team called family and friends and had them send money via a money app. They then used the money to buy mountains of canned food. Another team contacted a grocery store manager, told him what we were doing, and asked if they would donate. The manager graciously gave an entire pallet of canned goods. Other teams raided their home's food supply, while others went door to door. After all was said and done, my friends collected over 2500 cans of food in an hour.

We have been talking about our spiritual lives and cultivating something more generative. We have also been talking about how this kind of life affects how we relate to one another. I have learned time and again that those two truths strengthen each other. When I lovingly serve and give to others, it fills me even more. It is an astounding fact of life. I would even say that when you don't feel like you are cultivating anything generative in your life, the best place to start is by giving and serving others.

Question

As we embrace a spirit of generosity, what creative and impactful ways can you find to serve and support your community, particularly during times of need?

Week 75

In the Company of Heroes

Ten-year-old Isaac was diagnosed with Acute Myeloid Leukemia (AML) last summer. Having known his parents, Josh and Emily, for nearly fifteen years and having backpacked with his dad for almost as long, I remember when Isaac was born. They live in our neighborhood, and my daughters babysat him when he was younger.

In a divine turn of events, my oldest daughter, Anna, who works in oncology at Riley Children's Hospital, became one of Isaac's nurses throughout his treatment journey. Emily recalled those first moments from his Caring-Bridge page:

> When we were first admitted to Riley, we had a brief (less than 12 hours) stay on the 9th floor. They moved us to the 5th floor (oncology/hematology) the morning after we were admitted, right after Isaac's first bone marrow biopsy. Everything was so new and jarring. At that time, there were still a bunch of unknowns, and it was scary. When we rounded the corner on the 5th floor, the very first person we saw was the daughter of one of Josh's close friends who lives in our neighborhood! It felt like manna in the desert. God knows we are here, and he cares. He had a caring friend to greet us.

What the Browns discovered throughout Isaac's cancer treatment was that God used many caring friends among the nurses, doctors, and staff to support them, comfort them, and make their stay as pleasant and hopeful as possible.

Reflecting on the cast of characters that dot our lives and impact us meaningfully, it becomes clear how much of a blessing it is to be surrounded by those people while we have the chance to enjoy their presence. Watching the video of Isaac walking down the hallway for the last time, surrounded by his family and healthcare friends cheering for him, it was impossible not to be deeply moved.

More than ever, I understand how much we need each other. Not just to encourage and support us in our best times but also to lift us and stand by our side during our worst times. The journey of Isaac's recovery reminds us of the incredible power of community and love in healing. Watching Isaac's triumphant walk down the hospital hallway, it's clear that every cheer, every smile, and every tear shed in joy was a testament to the strength we derive from one another. This moment wasn't just a celebration of Isaac's victory over cancer; it was a profound acknowledgment of how deeply interconnected our lives are and how much richer and more resilient we become when we face life's challenges together.

Question

How can I actively strengthen my contributions to the supportive networks in my life and foster a more caring and resilient community, particularly for those enduring difficult periods?

Week 76

THE NOT VERY NEIGHBORLY
LESSON

WE HAVE LIVED IN our Sandy Hook neighborhood for over twenty years. Many good people have come and gone during that time, either by moving or passing away. I was recently reminded of some next-door neighbors we had when we first moved in—an older gentleman and his wife, both in their late 90s.

After a few years of living in our house and while I was at work, the near centenarian ambled to our back door and rapped on the glass with his wooden cane. When my wife greeted him and exchanged pleasantries, he told her I was "not very neighborly." Yes, that was the point of his visit—to let Jenny know that her husband was not neighborly.

Of course, when I got home from work, I was surprised by the visit and accusation. But not being one to immediately dismiss anyone's perspective, especially one's negative view of me, I meditated on the charge. I thought about how I would frequently put his garbage cans away without him knowing and greet him when we were outside. While I felt his view of being neighborly was limited, I knew what he wanted—a longer, sit-down visit from me. He wanted to get to know me. But I did not want to give him the time or the investment. Tough words to admit. Tough words to put on paper.

This past Saturday, Jenny and I went to one of the local high schools, Columbus North, to see my niece graduate. Unfortunately, the graduation took longer than we expected, and Jenny had to leave so she could prepare for graduation at Columbus East, where she works. She took the car and left me behind to finish watching. Immediately after my niece received her diploma,

I walked out to the street corner and requested an Uber ride to get home. On the same street corner, a lady stood waiting for someone to pick her up.

"I can't believe how long it is taking my husband to get here," she said. I laughed and explained my unique situation about my wife taking the car to prepare for graduation and leaving me behind. She asked who my wife was, and I told her. She laughed and said she knew Jenny because they lived in our subdivision a few streets over. Then, she insisted I cancel my Uber ride so they could take me home.

As I eventually got into their car, I considered their kindness. But then I realized I only received their kindness because my wife knew them, not me. She knew Jenny because Jenny had spent time talking to her and getting to know her.

Gut punch.

While I would argue that I know more of my neighbors now than ever, I can't help but feel the weight of missed opportunities to know them more deeply. I could continue to hide behind my introversion or the culturally conditioned norm of social isolation and never have to know anyone who lives around me. But the truth is that those excuses are facades that obscure the fact that I am selfish with my time.

What I am learning, though, as I reflect on the old man at my back door, the kind neighbors who gave me a ride, and pushing myself into longer conversations with my neighbors recently, is that being neighborly goes beyond mere pleasantries and occasional acts of kindness. It's about being present, knowing the people around you, and genuinely caring about their lives. These interactions are the stitches in the fabric of our communities, weaving us closer together and making the fabric stronger, from giving advice to being a shoulder to cry on to investing in our children's lives. I may never be a world-class conversationalist, but I realize how much we need people in our lives and how much they need us.

Question

In what ways can I be more present and engaged with the people in my community to help strengthen the fabric of our connections?

Week 77

Embodying Community

DAY 1

Action: Identify a situation or relationship where your ego is at play and causing resistance or defensiveness.

Reflection Question: What specific patterns, beliefs, or experiences have led you to recognize the need for transformation in this area? How do these factors affect your current state and your desire for change?

DAY 2

Action: Reflect on what transformation means to you and how it differs from simple change.

Reflection Question: In what ways does viewing transformation as a holistic and profound shift, rather than a surface-level change, influence your commitment to this process? How does this understanding shape your expectations and actions?

DAY 3

Action: Choose a specific aspect of the area you identified where you want to begin the transformation process.

Reflection Question: How can breaking down the transformation process into smaller, manageable steps make it more achievable for you? What initial actions can you take to initiate transformation in this specific aspect?

DAY 4

Action: Begin applying your understanding of transformation to this area.

Reflection Question: How do your thoughts, emotions, and behaviors change as you start engaging in the transformation process? What surprises or insights have emerged from this practice so far?

DAY 5

Action: Assess and reflect on the outcomes of practicing transformation in this area.

Reflection Question: How has your practice of transformation influenced your overall sense of self and your interactions with others? What specific changes have you observed in your mindset, behaviors, and relationships?

DAY 6

Action: Reflect on areas where your ego still causes resistance and make necessary adjustments to remain open to personal growth.

Reflection Question: What challenges or obstacles have you encountered in your transformation journey, and how can you overcome them? How can you integrate the lessons learned into other areas of your life to support ongoing growth?

DAY 7

Action: Plan how you will continue to invite humility and openness into your daily life, especially in challenging situations.

Reflection Question: What specific practices or routines can you establish to ensure that transformation remains a central part of your daily life? How can you hold yourself accountable to maintain this focus and measure your progress over time?

WEEKLY WRAP-UP

Reflection: As you reflect on the week's experience, what have been the most significant moments of growth or transformation for you? How can you continue to build on these insights and apply them to other areas of your life and relationships to support ongoing personal evolution?

Epilogue

FINDING TRUE HAPPINESS

FROM THE TIME I walked into a shoe store's bathroom two years ago to this morning, sitting at the dining room table to write this, I have spent more hours contemplating this picture than almost any other picture I have ever seen. The photo shows a large mural painted on the side of a building, with the words "Before I Die" boldly displayed across the top. Below these words, the mural is divided into numerous blank lines, inviting passersby to complete the sentence with chalk. This interactive word mural allows individuals to express their hopes, dreams, and aspirations for what they wish to accomplish in their lifetime.

That is what first caught my attention. Scrawled in chalk, people finished the thought with bucket list items, revolutionary aspirations, comedic attempts, and significant life milestones such as getting married or having a baby. So many people from different places in life, expressing the one meaningful thing they want to do or experience before they die. Maybe no one put much thought into it other than what was at the top of my mind. Or that they wrote some words to make their friends laugh. But in the bottom right corner, one humble offering stood out to me- find true happiness. This particular aspiration stood out to me for a few reasons, but primarily for its inclusion of the word true. The author seems to be distinguishing between transient and fleeting happiness versus a deeper, more profound, and lasting happiness that we all seek.

I remember taking a final exam in philosophy at Hanover College. The professor instructed us to, and this is crazy: write a question and answer it. Talk about a daunting test. First, you must have a great question and then know enough from the semester to answer it. At eighteen years old, my question was: What constitutes true happiness in one's life? I know you are dying to know how I answered it. The truth is that I don't remember, but I did get a rare A on this exam. I remember drawing a circle representing wholeness and discussing various elements that come together to make us whole or less whole. And maybe that is what this series of personal reflections and philosophical musings, these weekly meditations, have been- writing about areas of our lives that can ultimately make us more whole and truly happy before we die.

In these reflections, we've explored the depths of our inner selves, the wounds we carry, and the transformative power of Divine Love. From the chaos of daily life to the profound moments of stillness, each weekly meditation has been an attempt to reconnect with the core of living a fulfilled and meaningful life. Whether learning to forgive, embracing vulnerability, or finding joy in the mundane, these writings have been a journey toward understanding that true happiness is not a *destination* but a *continuous process* of growth and self-discovery. It's about cultivating a compassionate heart, nurturing our souls, and embracing the wonder and beauty of life in all its forms. As I sit here today, reflecting on this journey with you, I realize that we find true happiness in the small, intentional acts of love, kindness, and presence that make us more whole and connect us to the Divine and each other.

It has been a pleasure traveling with you.

Peace,

Brandon

REFERENCES

Andress, B. (2023). *And So By Fire* [Novel]. Quoir.

Andress, B. (2017). *Beauty in the Wreckage: Finding Peace in the Age of Outrage*. Quoir.

Andress, B. (2021). *What Can't Be Hidden* [Novel]. Quoir.

Bonhoeffer, D. (1993). *Life Together: The Classic Exploration of Faith in Community*. HarperOne.

Burton, T. (Director). (2003). *Big Fish* [Film]. Columbia Pictures.

Foster, M. (Director). (2006). *Stranger Than Fiction* [Film]. Columbia Pictures.

Holpuch, A. (2022, June 2). "A sixth grader was bullied over her yearbook message. Strangers responded with kindness." *The Washington Post*.

Iron and Wine. (2004). "Passing Afternoon." On *Our Endless Numbered Days* [CD]. Sub Pop Records.

Kipling, R. (1919). *The Gods of the Copybook Headings*.

Lawrence, B. (Creator). (2020). *Ted Lasso* [TV Series]. Apple TV+.

Metallica. (1991). "My Friend of Misery." On *Metallica (The Black Album)* [CD]. Elektra Records.

Reed, J. (Producer). (2023). *Chimp Empire* [Documentary]. Keo Films. Netflix.

Rohr, R. (2011). *Falling Upward: A Spirituality for the Two Halves of Life*. Jossey-Bass.

Rohr, R. (2020). *God Uses Everything*. Center for Action and Contemplation. Retrieved from Center for Action and Contemplation.

Rohr, R. (2009). *What the Mystics Know: Seven Pathways to Your Deeper Self.* Crossroad Publishing Company.

Ryder, Anne, WTHR. *Shanda Sharer's Mother and Murderer Form Unlikely Alliance.* May 12, 2012. https://www.wave3.com/story/18573121/shanda-sharers-mother-and-murderer-form-unlikely-alliance/.

Sigur Rós. (1997). *Átta* [Album]. Fat Cat Records.

Spurlock, M. (2005). *30 Days* [TV series]. FX Networks.

Weir, P. (Director). (1998). *The Truman Show* [Film]. Paramount Pictures.

ALSO BY THE AUTHOR

Beauty in the Wreckage: Finding Peace in the Age of Outrage (2018)
What Can't Be Hidden (2021)
And So By Fire (2023)

To contact Brandon Andress for speaking engagements, please visit www.brandonandress.com.

Many Voices. One Message.

quoir.com